HURON COUNTY LIBRARY

Branch Lib

P9-CLH-028

DE

HURON COUNTY LIB

3 6492 0033564 4

2 6492 0033564 3

FOR KING AND EMPIRE

THE CANADIANS ON THE SOMME

September to November, 1916

A Social History and Battlefield Tour

by N. M. Christie

edited by S. Hickman

JUN 24 '97

© **NORM CHRISTIE**

All rights reserved. No part of this work covered by copyright herein may be reproduced or used in any form or by any means — graphic, electronic, or mechanical, without the prior written permission of the author.

For King and Empire
Volume: II
The Canadians on the Somme,
September to November 1916

ISBN 0-9699039-4-4

Copyright 1996

Published by: Bunker to Bunker Books
                   34 Blue Spruce Cres.
                   Winnipeg, MB. R2M 4C2

Distributed by: C.E.F. Books   Bunker to Bunker Books
                   P.O. Box 29123   34 Blue Spruce Cres.
                   3500 Fallowfield Rd.   Winnipeg,
                   Nepean,   MB, R2M 4C2
                   ON K2J 4A9

Other Books in the Series

Front cover picture: The grave of Serjeant L. Clarke, V.C., 2nd Canadian Infantry, Etretat, France. (Photo credit: S. Hickman)
Back cover picture: Battlefield artifacts recovered during a pleasant walk near Regina Trench in 1995

Printed and bound by Hignell Printing Ltd., Winnipeg, MB. Canada

TABLE OF CONTENTS

Live Shells on the Somme, 1995

(PHOTO N. CHRISTIE)

INTRODUCTION

THE CANADIANS IN THE BATTLE OF THE SOMME
1916

The Battle of the Somme is one of the few battles of The Great War that is still alive in memory. The hopeless slaughter of the cream of the 1914 volunteers — the enthusiastic amateurs — still holds the imagination of the British people.

On the first day of battle, July 1, 1916, 20,000 British soldiers died for minimal gain. In one fell swoop, the Kitchener's volunteers of Britain had been smashed and the worst day in the history of the British Army was recorded. In the days and weeks that followed, the British used massive barrages to attack heavily defended German trenches. They captured some, only to lose many to German counterattacks.

By August 1916, three Canadian Infantry divisions were operating in Flanders. All three had already paid the price for battle experience. The 1st Division had suffered in the gas attack at Ypres in 1915, the 2nd at St. Eloi Craters in April 1916 and the 3rd was decimated in the Battle of Mount Sorrel in June 1916.[1] The tales of the slaughterhouse of the Somme must have affected the troops of the Canadian Corps who were now ordered south. Both sides were being bled white.

The Canadians arrived on the Somme in September and relieved the Australians near Pozières. What they witnessed was a landscape like that of the moon, villages were obliterated and rotting corpses were strewn everywhere. At Pozières, 23,000 Australians had lost their lives, been wounded or gone missing.

On September 15, 1916, the Canadians attacked as part of a major offensive, using tanks for the first time in battle. Over the next two months Canadian troops attacked the German positions

---

[1] The 4th Division arrived in Belgium in August 1916 but was not yet battle worthy.

at Courcelette: Regina Trench, Hessian Trench and Desire Trench. Often they charged against uncut wire and always fought against the inevitable German counterattacks. More than 24,000 Canadians were killed, wounded or missing in the Battles of the Somme.

Today, amid the rolling fields of the pretty, rural river valley that is the Somme, behind the peaceful façade of the countryside known for its fishing and tranquility, are the scars of that war — some 400 military cemeteries. When our grandfathers were there 80 years ago, a German trench ran behind each contour of the land and the ground was studded with ribbons of barbed wire.

Imagining the hell that was the Somme in 1916 is impossible for us. The only evidence today of the ferocity of those battles is the harvest of steel from the farmers' fields. After 80 years, rusted shell fragments, thousands of shrapnel balls, bullets, buttons, grenades and bones still surface. Otherwise, those once infamous names of the muted victories of 1916, the Sugar Refinery, Courcelette, Regina Trench, Kenora Trench and the Quadrilateral are forgotten.

More than 8,000 Canadians paid with their lives for those futile victories and their legacy, our heritage, deserves to be remembered.

Both my grandfather and great-uncle fought on the Somme. As a private in the 8th Canadian Field Ambulance, Randall Christie removed the wounded, a horrifying and dangerous task. His brother John was a Sergeant with the Princess Patricia's Canadian Light Infantry (PPCLI) and fought at Courcelette. Both managed to survive the war.

It is their legacy, their contribution to Canada, and the contribution of thousands of others just like them to whom this book is dedicated. Our knowledge of what they did, what they fought for, keeps them alive in our memory.

GETTING THERE

This guide recommends Arras as your centre of operations for visiting the battlefields of the Somme, which are within 30 kilometres of the town. The battlefields of Vimy and Arras 1918 are less than eight kilometres from the Arras town centre.

Arras is used to accommodating tourists and provides the best facilities in the region; however, tourist authorities can provide details on bed and breakfast facilities near the Somme battlefields for a less-expensive alternative.

Arras is the capital of the Pas-de-Calais in northern France, 170 kilometres north of Paris and easily accessible from London. A two-hour drive to Dover, a 75-minute ferry ride or 35-minute Hovercraft journey to Calais, and a one-hour drive on the major Calais-to-Paris toll road will get you to Arras. You could take the rail link through the Channel Tunnel from London to Lille, which is 45 minutes northeast of Arras near the Belgian border. Arras is about 1.5 hours by road from Brussels. Check with the Tourist Board for details.

Rental cars are available in any of these cities and tourist offices can supply routes and details of hotels.

In Arras, English is generally spoken in the main hotels. Otherwise very little English is spoken. Brush up on your French before going.

In France, stores close between noon and 2:00 p.m. **always.** Be sure to obtain film and other necessities before closing! Stopping for a long lunch is a strict and revered tradition in continental Europe.

There are 3.5 French francs (1996) to one Canadian dollar. Currency and traveler's checks can be exchanged at any bank.

Always visit the Tourism Office to obtain information on accommodation or events of interest.

WHAT TO BRING

Weather is very changeable in this part of Europe. Days can start sunny and change quickly to rain, hail or even a sprinkling of snow. Above all, be prepared for wet weather.

Other than the obvious passport, traveler's checks and appropriate clothing, bring the following to ensure a successful trip:

- a bottle opener and cork screw

- binoculars

- a camera (with 100 and 200 ASA film)

- a compass

- rubber boots

- Institute geographique national map number 2407 Bapaume east, 1:25,000 (this can be obtained at most bookstores in Arras)

- Michelin map No. 53 (preferably the Commonwealth War Graves Commission overprint, showing all the cemeteries)

- reference books (do your research before departure)

ABOUT ARRAS

Although situated in the heart of the industrial north of France, Arras rests quietly and peacefully, with an air of grandeur and finesse reflected in its great cobbled squares. No factory chimneys here, only the elegance of tradition which the city's inhabitants have fiercely held onto through thousands of years of captivity and terror. Badly damaged during the first World War, the inhabitants of the capital of Artois restored their incompara-ble monuments, the Grand'Place, place des Héros (Petite-Place), the rue de la Taillerie and the Town Hall in their original Flemish Gothic style, which make Arras one of the most beautiful towns in the north of France.

Of Roman origin, Arras was a stronghold in Julius Caesar's day. It was originally built on Baudimont Hill, east of the Crinchon Stream which runs through the town and called Atrebatum after a tribe which lived in the area, the Atrebates. Arras is a corruption of that name.

In the 5th century, during the reign of the Frankish king, Clovis I, Christianity was preached by Saint-Vaast, who created the diocese of Arras and was its first bishop. The most important abbey in the region was built in the 600s to honor the saint. A new town gradually emerged under the protection of this powerful monastery and eventually separated from the original construction by a continuous line of fortifications. By the 11th century, the two communities were quite independent of each other, each with its own form of government. The older Roman city on Baudimont Hill was the Cité of Arras and was under the jurisdiction of the bishop. The other, to the west, was the Ville proper and a dependency of the St. Vaast Abbey. While the Ville grew steadily, the Cité gradually declined until the mid-18th century when it was incorporated in the Ville.

Until Arras became part of the kingdom in France in the mid-17th century, the "Ville", as the capital of the County of Artois, successively belonged to the Counts of Flanders (850-1180), to the Counts of Artois (1180-1384), to the Dukes of Burgundy

(1384-1492) and finally to the Kings of Spain (1492-1640). The French kings often interfered in the affairs of Arras throughout this period. The town was besieged four times by the kings of France in the 9th and 10th centuries. In the 14th century, Arras was torn by popular sedition. Under the Dukes of Burgundy, and especially under Philippe-le-Bon, the town's world-renowned cloth and tapestry industries enjoyed a period of great prosperity. Its Arrazi tapestries became famous.

Arras is also infamous for imprisoning Joan of Arc during October and November 1430.

When Louis XI tried to claim Artois in 1477, the Cité of Arras promptly opened its gates to the Royal Army, but the Ville refused to surrender and was only conquered in 1479, after a long siege. Furious at the people's resistance, Louis XI exiled all the inhabitants and brought in the "Ligeriens." Arras became Spanish and its name was changed to Franchise. A few months later, the people of Arras were allowed to return to their homes, and in 1483, its ancient name, armorial bearings and laws were restored.

The inhabitants of Arras resisted French domination for years following the incident with Louis XI. They opened their gates to the German and Burgundian troops of Austria in 1492, only to regret doing so when the Germans pillaged and rifled their valuables

The Spanish-controlled city again came under the rule of the kings of France in the mid-17th century, when it fell after a long and bloody siege. The bombardments caused great damage to the abbey. A decade or so later, the town held out heroically against a Spanish invasion for 45 days.

Birth place of Augustin Robespierre, Arras was not spared during the Revolution. In 1793, Joseph Le Bon, sent there on a mission, organized the Terror. The guillotine was permanently erected in the Place de la Comédie. Travellers avoided Arras and the local merchants stopped doing business.

During the Great War, the Germans occupied Arras for only three days, September 6-9, 1914. But after their departure, the "Martyrdom of Arras" began. The Germans remained at the gates of the city until April 1917. Bombardment began October 6, 1914. Gunners fired ceaselessly on the military quarters and the two famous squares. The Hôtel de Ville, the Abbey of Saint Vaast and the Cathedral were burnt down, the belfry destroyed and by April 1917, Arras was completely in ruins. In March 1918, when the great German Offensive began, the bombardments broke out afresh, inhabitants were evacuated and by the end of August, the British drove the enemy out for good.

A visit to Arras should begin in the architecturally-unique Grand'Place, once an orchard belonging to the Abbey of Saint Vaast, and the Petite-Place. These squares have been bordered with gabled private houses and edged with stone columns and elliptical arches supporting vaulted galleries for hundreds of years.

Merchants once drew crowds of buyers to their stalls under the porticos of the squares and famous tapestries of Arras were once made in the damp cellars under the galleries.

Both squares were in ruin after the First World War. They were rebuilt in the original Flemish style.

Bordering the west side of the Petite-Place is the Hôtel de Ville, above which rises the graceful silhouette of the belfry. Long the centre of town, the Petite-Place attracted the townspeople to public meetings, festivals and public executions.

Today, the tourist office is located at the Hôtel de Ville (21 51 26 95) and is open daily. From there, guided tours can be arranged of the underground tunnels beneath the town hall (35 minutes, year-round). First used as cellars, the tunnels often served as shelters for the population during the invasions and for the soldiers of the First World War. You can also visit the belfry.

Two-hour tours of the town are also offered by guide-lecturers of the National Association for Historical Sites and Buildings daily in July and August at 3:00 p.m. and Wednesdays and Saturdays in June and September at 3:00 p.m. Reserve at the tourist office. Note, most museums in France are open from 10:00 a.m. to noon and 2:00 to 6:00 p.m. and closed on Tuesdays. Sunday and winter hours may be reduced. Abbey tel. 21 71 26 43.

Arras is famous for its "cobalt blue" porcelain, first produced in the late 18th century. It is available in most tourist shops in the town centre.

Accommodation is not a problem in Arras. You may want to check out the following hotels:

Astoria, 10 place Foch, 62000 Arras, tel. 21 71 08 14;

Hôtel Ibis, place Viviani, 62000 Arras, tel. 21 23 61 61;

Mercure Hôtel (3-star), 58 boulevard Carnot, 62000 Arras, tel. 21 23 88 88;

Hôtel Moderne, 1 boulevard Faidherbe, 62000 Arras, tel. 21 23 39

Ostel des 3 Luppars, 47 Grand'Place, 62000 Arras, tel. 21 07 41 41;

Hôtel de l'Univers, 5 place Croix Rouge, 6200 Arras, tel. 21 71 34 01.

Some eating establishments to consider are the restaurant at the Astoria which serves traditional French cuisine, tel. 21 71 29 78; or *La Faisanderie,* 45 Grand'Place (opposite 3 Luppars), tel. 21 48 20 76. As well, there is a variety of restaurants and cafés at the station square.

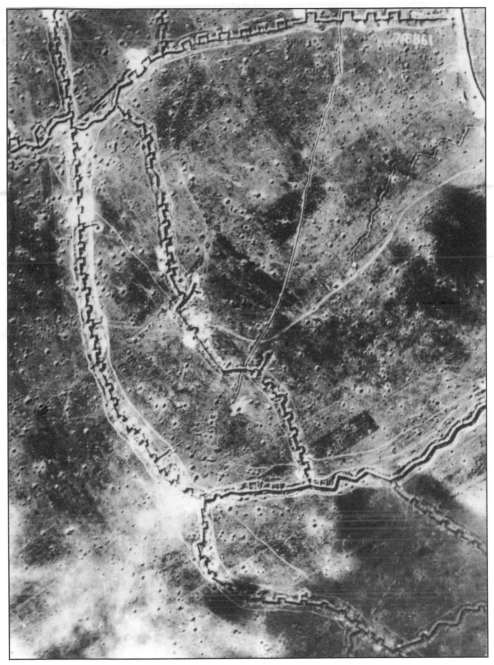

Aerial Photograph of Stuff Redoubt

(PUBLIC ARCHIVES C43989)

COMPONENTS OF THE CANADIAN EXPEDITIONARY FORCE
SOMME 1916

1ST CANADIAN DIVISION

1st Infantry Brigade	2nd Infantry Brigade	3rd Infantry Brigade
1st Battalion (Western Ontario)	5th Battalion (Saskatchewan)	13th Battalion Black Watch of Montreal)
2nd Battalion (Eastern Ontario)	7th Battalion (British Columbia)	14th Battalion (Royal Montreal Regiment
3rd Battalion (Toronto Regiment)	8th Battalion (90th Rifles of Winnipeg)	15th Battalion (48th Highlanders of Toronto)
4th Battalion (Central Ontario)	10th Battalion (Alberta)	16th Battalion (Canadian Scottish)

2ND CANADIAN DIVISION

4th Infantry Brigade	5th Infantry Brigade	6th Infantry Brigade
18th Battalion (Western Ontario)	22nd Battalion (Canadien-Français)	27th Battalion (City of Winnipeg)
19th Battalion (Central Ontario))	24th Battalion (Victoria Rifles of Montreal)	28th Battalion (Saskatchewan)
20th Battalion (Central Ontario)	25th Battalion (Nova Scotia)	29th Battalion (British Columbia)
21st Battalion (Eastern Ontario)	26th Battalion (New Brunswick)	31st Battalion (Alberta)

3RD CANADIAN DIVISION

7th Infantry Brigade	8th Infantry Brigade	9th Infantry Brigade
Royal Canadian Regiment	1st Canadian Mounted Rifles (Saskatchewan)	43rd Battalion (Cameron Highlanders of Winnipeg)
Princess Patricia's Canadian Light Infantry	2nd Canadian Mounted Rifles (British Columbia)	52nd Battalion (Northern Ontario)
42nd Battalion (Black Watch of Montreal)	4th Canadian Mounted Rifles (Central Ontario)	58th Battalion (Central Ontario)
49th Battalion (Alberta)	5th Canadian Mounted Rifles (Quebec)	60th Battalion (Victoria Rifles of Montreal)

4TH CANADIAN DIVISION

10th Infantry Brigade	11th Infantry Brigade	12th Infantry Brigade
44th Battalion (Manitoba)	54th Battalion (British Columbia)	38th Battalion (Eastern Ontario)
46th Battalion (Saskatchewan)	75th Battalion (Mississauga Horse)	72nd Battalion (Seaforth Highlanders of Vancouver)
47th Battalion (British Columbia)	87th Battalion (Grenadier Guards of Montreal)	78th Battalion (Winnipeg Grenadiers)
50th Battalion (Alberta)	102nd Battalion (North British Columbians)	73rd Battalion (Black Watch of Montreal)

CHART OF A DIVISION

(PUBLIC ARCHIVES OF CANADA C46□6)

The Canadians on the Somme, 1916

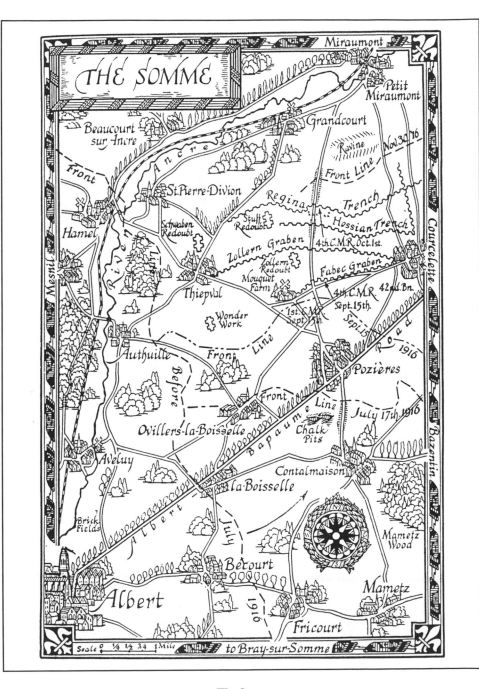

The Somme

THE BATTLE OF THE SOMME
July to November 1916

HISTORICAL OVERVIEW

The Battle of the Somme opened on July 1, 1916 with a British attack launched over a 20-kilometre front. Ushered in with a two-week bombardment of the German positions, the involved British divisions expected the July offensive to be successful. They were on the way to Berlin!

But the strategy of a heavy barrage, followed by a general assault, failed. The British Army, on July 1 alone, suffered 60,000 casualties, including 20,000 dead. The shock of this enormous tragedy still holds a place in the consciousness of the British people.

The attack north of the Albert-Bapaume road from Ovillers to Commecourt was a complete failure. South of the road, where the German lines swung in an easterly direction, the village of Fricourt was captured and the German defences in this "underbelly" pierced.

British forces continued their attacks to the north throughout July and August, slowly driving forward against heavy German opposition and numerous counterattacks.

By the end of August, the fighting south of and along the Bapaume-Albert road had reached the outskirts of Pozières, the highest point on the road. The fighting was severe in the area around Pozières. Australian forces painfully and expensively drove the Germans from the village, then pushed north and east toward Mouquet Farm and Courcelette. The eastern drive met heavy opposition and yielded little ground. The windmill, on the high point directly east of the village, was reached by the end of August.

Meanwhile, the Canadian Corps was ordered to the battlefield of the Somme at the end of August. The 1st, 2nd and 3rd
Canadian Infantry Divisions[2] had passed July and August in the
always dangerous Yprès Salient. There, in spite of there being
no major action, a thousand Canadian lives had been lost.

With summer coming to a close, the 1st Canadian Division
was moved to the Somme and attached to the II Australian Army
Corps. The Pozières front was being heavily contested by both
sides when they entered the line on September 2/3.

As the Somme battlefield lacked any particularly advanta-
geous physical characteristics, the Germans had built a complex
series of interconnecting trenches and deep redoubts across the
rolling chalk hills. They took full advantage of every contour.

To protect themselves from observation, the Germans
generally dug in on the down side of a slope. The trenches were
deep and solid, often strategically interconnected with other
switch trenches. A warren of communication and support
trenches were used for transporting supplies, reinforcements
and ammunition. The Redoubt positions were often connected
by tunnels coming from a variety of places in the support lines. In
front of the trenches were belts of barbed wire.

The major German trenches of Fabeck, Regina, Kenora,
Sugar and Candy ran across the valley north of Pozières and
Courcelette. Mouquet Farm was heavily fortified and connected
by a complex system of tunnels leading to the German support
positions.

Between September 4 and 7, the 1st Canadian Division's 16th
Battalion (Canadian Scottish) supported the Australian Infantry
attack on Mouquet Farm and other German positions north of
Pozières. The Canadian battalion suffered 349 causalities.

On September 9, the 1st Canadian Infantry Brigade attacked
a German trench work south of the Pozières windmill. In this
attack, Corporal Leo Clarke of the 2nd Battalion (Eastern

---

[2] The 4th Canadian Division arrived in France in August 1916, but did not join the
Canadian Corps until after the Somme Battles. However, it was heavily involved in
the Somme Battle in October and November 1916 as part of the British Army Corps.
Its first major battle was on the Somme.

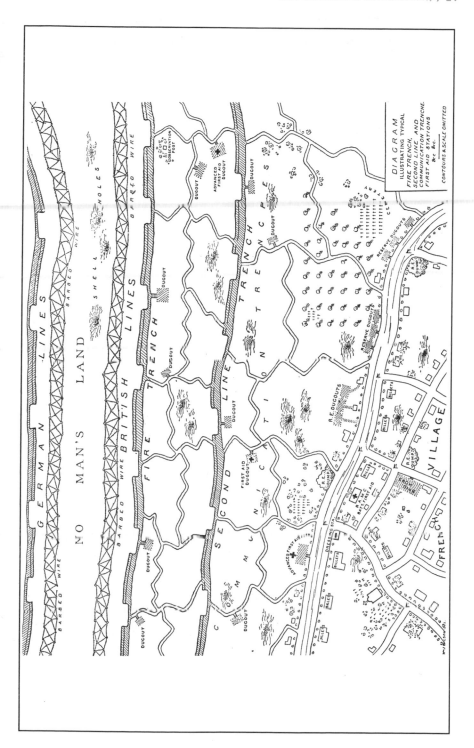

Schematic Trench System 1916

Ontario) won the Victoria Cross. These actions were minor but costly.

The first main fighting ground for the Canadians came on September 15 at the Battle of Flers-Courcelette. Part of a general British attack, this was the first time in the history of warfare that tanks were employed. At 6:20 a.m. on September 15, the 2nd Canadian Division attacked astride the Albert-Bapaume road.

Its leading battalions (right to left) were the 18th (Western Ontario), the 20th (Central Ontario), 21st (Eastern Ontario), 27th (City of Winnipeg) and 28th (Saskatchewan). They quickly broke through the German front lines and advanced on their objectives. On the right, Candy Trench fell quickly to the 18th and 20th Battalions.

After heavy fighting, the Sugar Refinery fell to the 21st Battalion. The tanks helped but did not greatly improve the infantry attack.

To the left of the 2nd Canadian Division, the 3rd Division met with similar success in breaching the German front lines. The 5th Canadian Mounted Rifles (Quebec) covered the 2nd's left flank and captured the northern extension of Sugar Trench. The 1st Canadian Mounted Rifles (Saskatchewan) advanced into Mouquet Farm. In the late afternoon the 22nd (Quebec) and the 25th (Nova Scotia) Battalions exploited the earlier successes by attacking north from Candy Trench into Courcelette. In fierce hand-to-hand fighting, they captured the village.

On the 3rd Division's front, the 42nd (Black Watch of Montreal), 49th (Edmonton) and PPCLI established a foothold in Fabeck Graben.

The first day of battle had been successful for the Canadian Corps.

Over the next few days the 3rd division captured Fabeck Graben and tried to reach the next major trench system at Zollern Graben, but with little success.

Meanwhile, in Courcelette, the 1st Division (which had replaced the 2nd Division) made small inroads on the heights north of the village

On September 26, the Battle of Thiepval Ridge began. The 1st Canadian Division assaulted the German trenches that spread across the Ancre valley west of Courcelette. Right to left, the 14th (Royal Montreal Regiment), 15th (48th Highlanders of Toronto), 5th (Saskatchewan) and 8th (90th Rifles of Winnipeg — The Little Black Devils) Battalions successfully captured Zollern Graben and tried to push on to Hessian Trench, 600 metres to the north. They managed to reach Regina Trench (a third main German Trench 500 metres north of Hessian Trench) but were unable to hold it. They completed the capture of Hessian Trench the following day.

The 2nd Division attacked out of Courcelette village on September 26. The 31st (Alberta) and 29th (British Columbia) Battalions pushed north with limited success. The next day the Germans retreated to Regina Trench leaving the cemetery, Death Valley and the heights north of the village to the Canadians.

On October 1, the 2nd Canadian Division made the first attempt to take Regina Trench. Too rushed, the attack failed, but the battalions managed to capture portions of Kenora Trench, a main switch trench connected to Regina Trench.

They attacked from the remnants of Hessian Trench, right to left, the 22nd, 25th, 24th (Queen Victoria's Rifles of Montreal), 4th Canadian Mounted Rifles and 5th Canadian Mounted Rifles of the 3rd Division attacked. They made few inroads, however, as uncut wire left the infantry exposed to machine gun fire.

The Canadians' largest assault on Regina Trench came on October 8, from Destremont Farm to Kenora Trench. Although eight battalions were involved, the attack was ill-prepared and artillery bombardment left the German wire undamaged.

On the left, the 49th, Royal Canadian Regiment, 43rd (Cameron Highlanders of Winnipeg), and 58th (Central Ontario) Battalions were stopped by the Germans or driven back by concentrated counterattacks. On the far right, the 3rd

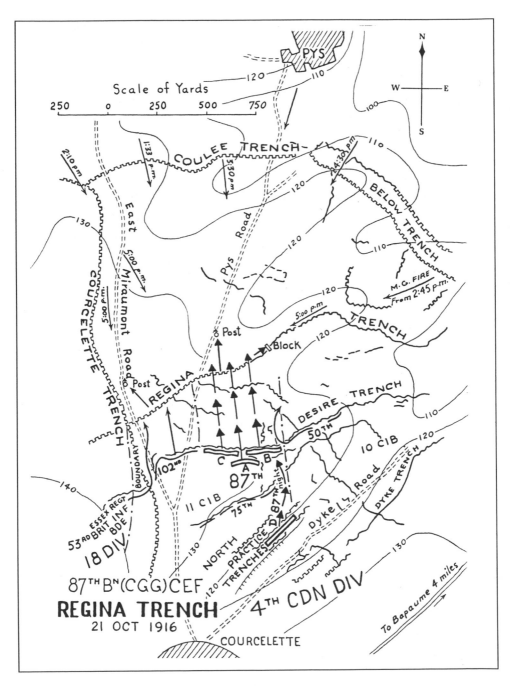

The Third Assault on Regina Trench

(CANADIAN GRENADIER GUARDS)

(Toronto Regiment) and 4th (Central Ontario) broke into the Quadrilateral near Le Sars and linked with the 16th Battalion in Regina Trench.

Nevertheless, the attack of the 13th (Black Watch of Montreal) had failed in the face of uncut wire. Unable to support the successful troops, they retreated on October 9. Another ill-prepared attack on Regina trench had failed with disastrous consequences. The Canadian Corps withdrew from the Somme battle after this attack, counting its losses at 20,000 killed, wounded and missing.After the success of September 15, the Canadians, much like the British troops, had been unable to follow up.

The 4th Canadian Division came into the line in mid-October 1916 and launched its first main attack of the war on Regina Trench on October 21. The 87th (Grenadier Guards of Montreal) and 102nd (North British Columbians) managed to secure a footing in Regina Trench between the East Miraumont and Pys roads, but the balance of the trench remained in German hands. On October 25, the 44th Battalion (Winnipeg) launched a further attack on Regina east of the Pys road, but again uncut wire and hasty planning resulted in catastrophic losses for the new unit, and no gains.

On November 11, the 4th Division threw three battalions at the nearly-obliterated Regina Trench.

The 102nd, 47th (British Columbia) and 46th (Saskatchewan) succeeded in capturing the longest German Trench ever constructed on the Western Front. It had taken the Canadians 42 days!

On November 18 the 4th Division's 38th Battalion (Eastern Ontario), 87th, 54th (Kootenay), 75th (Mississauga Horse) and 50th (Alberta) succeeded in capturing Desire Trench, 400 metres north of the obliterated Regina Trench. The 38th and 87th broke through and advanced to Grandcourt Trench, but were later forced to withdraw.

The Battle of the Somme was over. The Canadians had suffered more than 8,000 dead for a gain of 2.5 kilometres of mutilated chalky Somme farmland.

The 4th Division was relieved at the end of November and joined the other three Canadian Infantry Divisions in the Canadian Corps in front of Vimy Ridge.

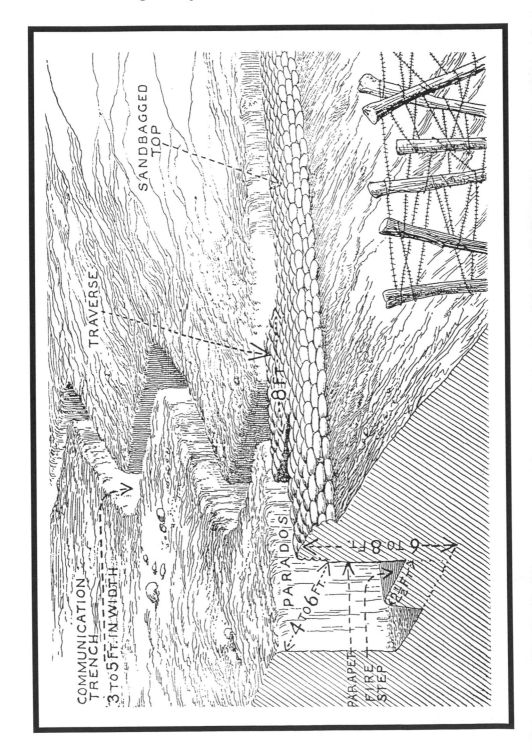

TOUR ITINERARY:
Duration 4 Hours

THE BATTLE OF THE SOMME —
September to November 1916

Point 1:   *The jump-off line of September 15, 1916*

Point 2:   *The capture of Courcelette Village, September 15, 1916*

Point 3:   *The capture of Fabeck and Zollern Graben, September 1916*

Point 4:   *Mouqet Farm, September 1916*

Point 5:   *The attacks on Regina Trench — the left attacks, September to November 1916*

Point 6:   *Death Valley*

Point 7:   *The capture of Regina and Desire Trenches, November 1916*

Point 8:   *The Quadrilateral — the right flank, October to November 1916*

THE BATTLE OF THE SOMME

THE TOUR

The tour begins at the Grand'Place in Arras. Leave the square in a southeasterly direction to Bapaume and Peronne on Highway N17. Immediately upon reaching Bapaume (22 kilometres from Arras), turn right onto the first main road, the D929, towards Albert.

You will pass Warlencourt British Cemetery on the left after four kilometres, and arrive at the village of Le Sars after another two kilometres. Continue for another five kilometres to the Canadian Monument at Courcelette. As you ascend the hill beyond the monument, watch for signs for the Australian Windmill Memorial on the right side of the road at Pozières. Stop and enter the memorial park. Walk to the northeast corner.

Point 1: The jump-off line of September 15, 1916

Throughout July and August 1916, the Australians battled their way through Pozières village and to the point where you now stand. It was at the windmill, the highest point on the Pozières Ridge, that the Australians fought hand-to-hand with the Germans and, as the inscription on the memorial states, "fell thicker than on any field of battle in the war."

In early September, the first Canadian units entered the Somme battle, occupying trenches recently captured by the Australians. Look to the north, northeast and to the east for views of the entire Canadian battlefield of the Somme. Perhaps you can imagine in the valley before you the ribbons of chalk spoil that marked the German trenches and the belts of uncut barbed wire that protected them.

The infamous Mouquet Farm, where the 16th Battalion first supported the Australians, is about a kilometre northwest. The farm itself has been rebuilt almost exactly where the original farm was. The attack, which took place between September 4 and 7, was unsuccessful. The Germans had connecting tunnels joining various defensive positions and effectively surprised the attackers by popping up behind them after they thought the

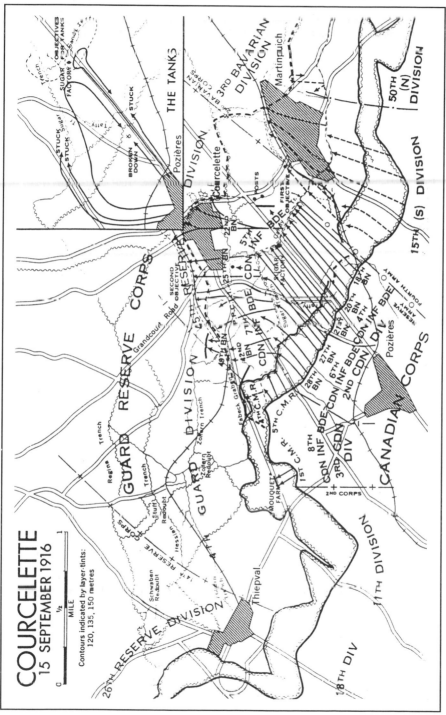

(DEPARTMENT OF NATIONAL DEFENSE)

Jump-Off September 15, 1916

COURCELETTE
15 SEPTEMBER 1916

Contours indicated by layer-tints:
120, 135, 150 metres

MILE

THE TANKS

SUGAR FOR TANKS
SUGAR FACTORY
OBJECTIVES

STUCK
STUCK
STUCK
STUCK Sugar
Alley
BROKEN DOWN

Trench

Pozières

Courcelette

3RD BAVARIAN DIVISION

Martinpuich

50TH (N) DIVISION

15TH (S) DIVISION

FIRST CDN OBJECTIVE

POSTS

RESERVE FOURTH ARMY

SUGAR FACTORY

GUARD RESERVE CORPS

RESERVE DIVISION

SECOND OBJECTIVE

5TH DIVISION

Grandcourt Road

49TH BN

42ND BN

P.P.C.L.I.

25TH BN

22ND BN

5TH CDN INF

7TH CDN INF BDE

18TH BN

20TH BN

21ST BN

4TH CDN INF BDE

27TH BN

28TH BN

6TH CDN INF BDE

2ND CDN INF DIV

Pozières

CANADIAN CORPS

GUARD DIVISION

Fabeck Graben

Zollern Trench

Zollern Redoubt

Regina Trench

Trench

Stuff Redoubt

Hessian

Schwaben Redoubt

14TH RESERVE CORPS

26TH RESERVE DIVISION

MOUQUET FARM

1ST C.M.R.

4TH C.M.R.

5TH C.M.R.

8TH CDN INF BDE

3RD CDN INF DIV

2ND CORPS

11TH DIVISION

18TH DIV

Thiepval

position had been cleared. A subsequent attack on September 15 by the 1st Battalion Canadian Mounted Rifles was somewhat successful, but the farm was not finally cleared until September 26.

To the west is the Thiepval Ridge, marked by the distinctive Thiepval Memorial to the Missing (listing 72,000 names of British and South African soldiers with no known grave). The ridge was first attacked, with disastrous results, on July 1, 1916. It was finally captured on September 26.

In the middle distance, to the south of Mouquet Farm, were the German trenches connecting the farm to Courcelette, which the 2nd Battalion (Eastern Ontario) fought to capture on September 4. On September 9 they captured the German trenches in front of Martinpuich (the village south of Courcelette) in an assault that took place southeast of the park across the Albert-Bapaume road. The trench system ran southeasterly roughly 500 metres from where you stand.

Corporal Leo Clarke of Winnipeg won the Victoria Cross in this action.[3] When Clarke and a section of bombers were attacked by 20 Germans, Clarke advanced toward them, emptied his revolver at them, then picked up two German rifles to continue the assault. He pursued the fleeing enemy, shot four more and captured a fifth.

Courcelette sits in a hollow to the northeast. The village, 1.5 kilometres behind the German lines, was the main objective of the Canadian attack of September 15.

North across the valley was Fabeck Graben, the main German trench link to Sugar and Candy Trenches and the Mouquet Farm defences to the west. Courcelette British Cemetery, 1,250 metres north of you in the valley, marks the Fabeck Graben Trench.

You are standing at the 2nd Canadian Division's jump-off position of September 15. At 6:20 a.m., the Canadians attacked on both sides of the Albert-Bapaume road. The 18th Battalion,

---

[3] Clarke was wounded in the attack on Regina Trench and died a few days later at Etretat, south of Dieppe on the French coast, at the age of 24. Clarke was one of three men living on the same block in Winnipeg who won the Victoria Cross. The others were CSM F. W. Hall (posthumous) and Captain R. Shankland. The Winnipeg street was subsequently renamed Valour Road.

on right, attacked towards Martinpuich. The 20th and 21st Battalions straddled the road and the 27th and 28th Battalions advanced toward Courcelette. The fighting was severe, but within 15 minutes the five battalions broke through the German front lines, assaulted the main German defence line in front of Courcelette village (i.e. Candy and Sugar Trenches), pushed the Attack to the Sugar Refinery (now a garden store) on the Albert-Bapaume road, and swerved north toward Courcelette.

In the second phase, the 22nd and 25th Battalions pushed through and captured the village of Courcelette (see *Point 2*).

Meanwhile, the 3rd Division attacked to the left of the 2nd Division, hitting German defences in the hollow west of Courcelette, and driving into the main German trenches, principally Fabeck Graben.

On the extreme left of the Canadian line, the 1st Canadian Mounted Rifles attacked Mouquet Farm. Support battalions of the 3rd Division, the 49th, 42nd and the PPCLI, followed through the captured trenches and attacked the Fabeck Graben Trench west of the village *(Point 3)*.

Try to imagine the 15,000 Canadian soldiers surging ferociously forward along the line amid gun fire and continuous artillery fire. In spite of the odds, September 15 was a very successful day by 1916 standards.

The battle of Flers-Courcelette marked the first use of tanks. The 2nd Division received six tanks for its attack, but the effect was small. Only one achieved its objective and four were put out of action by artillery. The memorial to this first tank action is directly across the road from the Pozières Windmill Australian Memorial.

Head back toward Bapaume on the Albert-Bapaume road. Stop after 1.5 kilometres at the Canadian Memorial Park at Courcelette.

COURCELETTE CANADIAN MEMORIAL

The Canadian monument on the Albert-Bapaume road, south of Courcelette village, stands on one of eight First World War Canadian battlefields officially commemorated.

In 1920, the Canadian Battlefield Monument Commission decided to erect memorials at:

St. Julien — to commemorate the Second Battle of Ypres

Hill 62 — to commemorate the Battle of Mount Sorrel

Courcelette — to commemorate the Battle of the Somme

Vimy — to commemorate the Battle of Vimy Ridge

Passchendaele — to commemorate the Battle of Passchendaele

Le Quesnel — to commemorate the Battle of Amiens

Dury — to commemorate the Battle of Arras 1918 and the capture of the Drocourt-Queant line

Bourlon Wood — to commemorate the Battles of the Canal du Nord, Cambrai, the capture of Valenciennes and Mons and the March to the Rhine

It was decided that Vimy would act as the National Memorial and have a unique design. The other seven would be marked with identical memorials.

A competition was held to choose an architect to design the monuments. Walter Allward of Toronto was chosen for Vimy's unique memorial and Frederick C. Clemesha of Regina took second place.

Clemesha's design, "The Brooding Soldier," was built at St. Julien and had such a stark effect at its unveiling in 1923 that the Monument Commission decided it also should remain unique.

In conjunction with the architectural advisor, P. E. Nobbs, the cube design was developed for the remaining six monuments. A 13-tonne block of Stanstead granite was used for each. A wreath was carved into two sides of the monument and on the other two sides was engraved a brief explanation of the exploits of the Canadian Corps in that specific battle. One side is in English, the other in French.

At Courcelette, the monument reads:

THE CANADIAN CORPS BORE A VALIANT PART IN FORCING BACK
THE GERMANS ON THESE SLOPES
DURING THE BATTLES OF THE SOMME
SEPT. 3RD-NOV. 18TH, 1916

Around the base of the stone, it reads:

HONOUR TO CANADIANS WHO ON THE FIELDS OF FLANDERS
AND OF FRANCE FOUGHT IN THE CAUSE OF THE ALLIES WITH
SACRIFICE AND DEVOTION

These words hardly represent the sacrifice and suffering of the 8,000 men who were killed here. They could not satisfy the mothers and wives whose loved ones vanished on those chalky slopes.

Point 2: The capture of Courcelette Village, September 15, 1916

Look down the road toward Albert. This is where the 2nd Canadian Division advanced.

Candy, the main German trench, crossed the road 250 metres to the west. Sugar Trench ran east-west midway between the road and Courcelette to a point one kilometre west of the Canadian monument. The clear field of fire and observation the Germans had is evident, and the destruction of the attacking Canadian troops by machine guns is not hard to imagine.

It was across the fields west of the Memorial Park that the 22nd and 25th Battalions surged to meet the German defenders in the rubble of Courcelette. Every inch of the advance was contested by the Germans through repeated counterattacks.

The sunken road east of the park, which leads into the village, was the scene of heavy fighting on September 15 and the days that followed, as the Canadians sought to improve their position by driving north and east of Courcelette.

Aerial Photograph of Courcelette During the Attack, September 15, 1916

(PUBLIC ARCHIVES OF CANADA PAC43987)

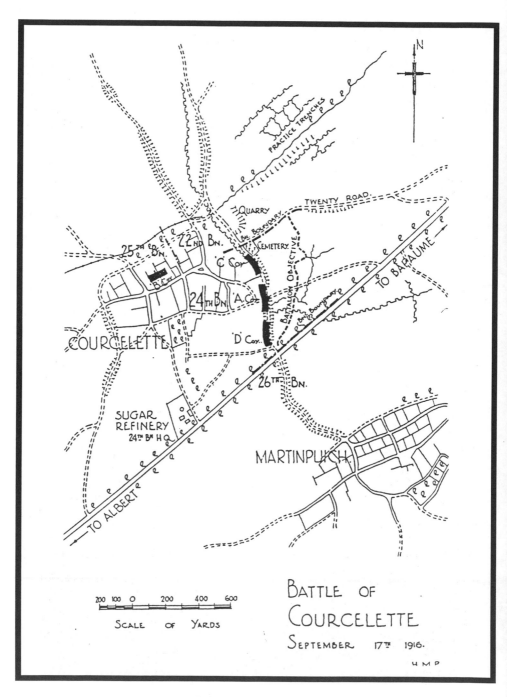

Local Action–Courcelette

*View of jump-off, September 15, 1916 from Courcelette British Cemetery
(the ridge across the horizon)*

(PHOTO N. CHRISTIE)

The Ruins of Courcelette

(PUBLIC ARCHIVES CANADA PAC26106)

Return to your car, continue about 50 or 60 metres along the main Albert-Bapaume road and turn left into the village of Courcelette. You will reach the village in about .5 kilometre. Turn left and continue straight through the village centre, exiting to the west. Follow the sign to Courcelette British Cemetery. Stop and enter the cemetery.

Point 3: The capture of Fabeck and Zollern Graben, September 1916

The communications tower and the flagpoles of the Australian Windmill Memorial are visible to the south along the Albert-Bapaume road. That was the jumping-off point of the Canadian Corps on September 15, 1916. The 21st, 27th and 28th Battalions swarmed to the attack across the fields in front of you, overrunning the front-line German trenches and capturing the second-line Sugar Trench. Sugar ran east-west across the fields midway between Courcelette British Cemetery and the Albert-Bapaume road.

After the initial success of the 2nd Divisions' attack, a second attack was launched against the next German position of Fabeck Graben Trench by the 3rd Division at 6:00 p.m. This trench ran east-west along the road that runs between the village and the cemetery. The 42nd, 49th and PPCLI Battalions broke into Fabeck Graben and tried to clear it of Germans. The defense was fierce and the units of the 3rd Division fought to a standstill. The Black Watch (42nd) assaulted Fabeck Graben near the cemetery (where you stand) and the PPCLI fought closer to the village. Simultaneously, the 22nd and 25th Battalions fought ferociously in the village.

With most of Fabeck Graben secured, at 8:30 p.m. the 49th leapfrogged the PPCLI and pushed onto the high ground north and northeast of the cemetery. They dug in about 300 metres north of the cemetery, but still 300 metres short of the next main German trench, Zollern Graben. A 100-metre section of Fabeck Graben, across from where you are standing, stubbornly resisted all attempts to dislodge it from German hands.

On the following day, the PPCLI and 49th Battalions attacked the enclave and succeeded in clearing the trench. During the action, Private John Chipman Kerr of the 49th

Battalion raced along the top of the trench shooting the enemy bombers. His action so surprised the hard-pressed Germans that 62 of their unwounded soldiers surrendered. Kerr was awarded the Victoria Cross for his bravery.[4]

The treetops of Mouquet Farm are visible west of the cemetery. It was there, the left of the Canadian line, that the 8th Infantry Brigade of the 3rd Canadian Division attacked. The 1st Canadian Mounted Rifles attacked northward into the farm and captured it after severe bombing and fighting.

The success was short-lived, however, as the Germans slipped back into the farm from underground tunnels and attacked from the Canadian rear. The farm was not cleared until September 26.

Approximately 700 metres west of the cemetery, the 4th Battalion Canadian Mounted Rifles (Toronto) and the 5th Canadian Mounted Rifles attacked the front line German trench and moved on to attack Fabeck Graben on the left of the Black Watch. The attack was marginally successful but achieved its major objective to protect the left flank of the new Canadian line.

Over the next five days, various local attacks improved the Canadian position. The objective was to secure a better jump-off position for attacking Zollern Graben, a strong, well-wired German trench running west from Courcelette, behind the rise north of Courcelette British Cemetery. It is a difficult position to see from the cemetery.

There are two options at this point in the tour. First, you can return to the village, turn left when Regina Trench Cemetery is signposted and stop after one kilometre, 500 metres from the cemetery (go to *Point 5*). Your second choice, if the road ahead is dry, is to continue along the twisting road for 1.2 kilometres toward Mouquet Farm (see *Point 4*).

---

[4] Kerr was born in Fox River, Nova Scotia, January 11, 1887. He died at Port Moody, British Columbia February 19, 1963.

WILLIAM WEBSTER WILSON
CAPTAIN, *1st Canadian Div. Sig. Corps, C.E.F.*

ERNEST ALFRED REYNOLDS
LIEUTENANT, *4th Battalion, C.E.F.*

Was born in Edinburgh, Scotland, in November, 1890. He was educated at James Gillespie's School in his native city. At the age of nineteen he entered the Royal Bank of Scotland, in Leith, where he remained for over four years. He then came to Canada and joined the staff of the Bank of Montreal, He enlisted in Western Canada with the Signalling Corps of the First Canadian Division in which he was given his commission as Lieutenant, and after successfully completing his qualifying course he went overseas with this unit. He was later promoted to the rank of Captain and was subsequently appointed Adjutant in his corps. In October, 1916, during the Canadian offensive on the Somme he was listed as "missing" after an enemy counter-attack, and in the following December he was definitely reported as having been killed in action.

Was born in London, England, in December, 1886. After receiving his education at the Westminster City School, he served for a time with the National Bank of India, Limited, in London. He then came to Canada where he joined the staff of the Bank of British North America, eventually becoming Manager of the branch in St. Catharines, Ontario. He enlisted in St. Catharines, in 1915, and was given his commission as Lieutenant in the 76th Battalion, Canadian Infantry. He went overseas with his unit and in July, 1916, he went to France where he was transferred to the 4th Battalion, Canadian Infantry. He moved at once with his battalion to the Somme battlefront for the offensive of 1916. Here he was instantly killed by enemy fire on the early morning of October 8th, 1916, while leading his platoon in an attack on the enemy position.

Valley of Regina Trench. (Regina Trench Cemetery, middle and Adanac Cemetery on horizon just right of Regina Trench Cemetery)

(PHOTO N. CHRISTIE)

View of Thiepval Memorial and Mouquet Farm

(PHOTO N. CHRISTIE)

Point 4: Mouquet Farm, September 1916

You are on the crest of a 150-metre ridge separating Mouquet Farm and Courcelette. The view of the Somme battlefield is excellent. Regina Trench Cemetery is to the northeast and Adanac Cemetery to its right, 2.8 kilometres distant. Regina Trench snaked its way across the valley between these two positions. Grandcourt is to the north and Miraumont to the right of Grandcourt, across the Ancre River. Thiepval Ridge and the Thiepval Memorial to the Missing are visible in the west. Pozières is 1.5 kilometres to the south.

The area on which you stand was vitally important to the Germans. A major German trench system ran along the ridge linking up with their major defences of Zollern Redoubt and Stuff Redoubt in the north. This in turn was linked to the German defences and the Schwaben Redoubt on Thiepval Ridge.

Mouquet Farm was attacked several times by the Australians in August 1916 and, with Canadian units, in early September. The 16th Battalion supported the Australian attack on this ridge. Gains were minuscule for such severe fighting. In this minor action, the battalion had the second worst casualties of the war.

Still, during the winter months, after the soil has been turned and exposed to a month's rain, evidence of the ferocity of the battle surfaces in the farmers' fields in the form of shrapnel balls, bullets, buttons and fragments of copper driving-bands. Even after 80 years!

After the attack of the 1st Canadian Mounted Rifles on September 15, described in *Point 3*, Mouquet Farm became the responsibility of British units. And what a deadly place it was!

The view east, of Courcelette and the fields to the north, is of the entire Canadian campaign on the Somme. The weaving of Regina, Hessian, Kenora, Zollern and Fabeck Trenches were visible from this point. Try to imagine the valiant attacks over open ground against these well-fortified, barbed-wired trenches. Prior to the attacks, heaven and earth would explode with massive artillery barrages extending from Thiepval Ridge beyond Courcelette. It was a nightmare.

Return to the village of Courcelette. Turn left on the signposted road to Regina Trench Cemetery. Ascend the ridge and stop at the crossroads, 1.1 kilometres along the road.

Point 5: The attacks on Regina Trench — the left attacks, September to November 1916

From this rise, Courcelette is visible to the southeast, Courcelette British Cemetery to the south and Regina Trench Cemetery to the north (also the village of Miraumont further north). The Germans were heavily dug-in along the valley between Courcelette and Miraumont in three main trench systems, Hessian, Regina and Grandcourt, as well as smaller trenches, all interconnected and heavily protected with barbed wire.

After the success of September 15, the Canadian Corps pushed north in an attempt to capture these main lines. Every metre of trench would have to be won in the face of deadly German machine guns, heavy artillery, barbed wire and counterattacks.

After the initial capture of Fabeck Graben (at Courcelette Cemetery), the Canadians drove on the east-west running trench of Zollern Graben 500 metres south of here. Those first attempts to take Zollern Graben on September 20 met with some success at the junction of the trench and the village of Courcelette. However, the attack on the centre by the 43rd Battalion had been driven back.

The next attempt by the 1st Canadian Division was to take place on September 26. Their ridiculously ambitious objective was to capture Zollern Graben, push north 600 metres, capture Hessian Trench (where you are standing) and continue 400 metres north over the rise to take Regina Trench.

The front of the Canadian attack, which ran from the east side of Courcelette (500 metres west of the electrical pylons) to an area one kilometre west of you, was known as the Battle of Thiepval Ridge. From right to left, the battalions were the 14th Royal Montreal Regiment, the 15th, the 5th and the 8th (The Little Black Devils). At 12:35 p.m. the Canadians, supported by the British 11th and 18th Divisions, surged forward, quickly over-ran Zollern Graben and drove 600 metres ahead into Hessian Trench. They suffered heavily from isolated German machine gun nests set up in No Mans Land and in the German wire.

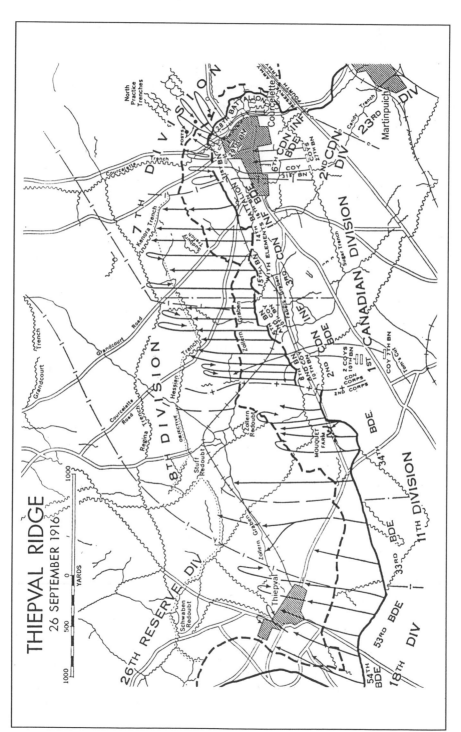

(DEPARTMENT OF NATIONAL DEFENSE)

Thiepval Ridge — The Attack September 26, 1916

On the left of the Canadian attack The Little Black Devils encountered severe machine gun fire from the left flank, unprotected because the British on the flank were unable to keep up with the Canadian advance. Although fire drove them back, the other Canadians were successful in capturing portions of Hessian Trench.

The 14th Battalion, with hard fighting, captured most of Kenora Trench, a strongly held position connecting Regina, Hessian and Courcelette Trenches, but was forced to withdraw on September 27. The fighting continued until September 29, Hessian Trench was finally secured and Regina Trench was within sight of the Canadian Corps.

On the right of the 1st Division, the 31st and 29th Battalions attacked German positions north of Courcelette and achieved limited success. On September 27, the 31st and 27th Battalions attacked again and discovered the Germans had withdrawn to Regina Trench, 900 metres north of their outposts. The territory east of Courcelette was left to the Canadians.

Regina Trench was one of the longest German trenches built on the Western Front, well protected by belts of barbed wire and with the distinct advantage of being in a gully on the down-side of a sharp rise. Bombarding it effectively was difficult, and observing it even more difficult. In addition, a ravine and a series of sunken roads connected it to the village of Grandcourt, making it easy to resupply.

The trench itself ran across the valley between Thiepval and Le Sars, 100 metres north of Regina Trench Cemetery. It followed the gully visible to the north, crossed the fields, past the Power Pylons and cut the west and east Miraumont roads and the Pys road 300 metres south of Adanac Cemetery (barely visible to the east).

By October 1, the 2nd and 3rd Canadian Divisions were prepared to capture Regina Trench in what would be the start of the Battle of the Ancre Heights. The Canadians had attacked continuously since the September 15 assault and preparations and artillery assistance had become insufficient to capture the German lines effectively. The Somme, like it had been for the

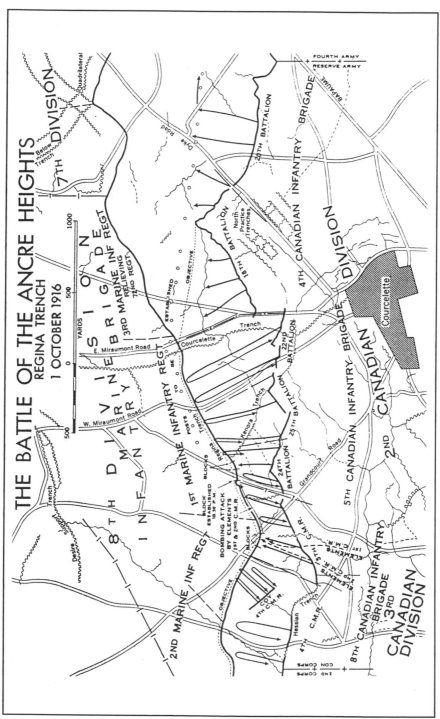

THE BATTLE OF THE ANCRE HEIGHTS

REGINA TRENCH

1 OCTOBER 1916

(DEPARTMENT OF NATIONAL DEFENSE)

The First Assault on Regina Trench

British and Australians, became a battle of attrition for the Canadians. High losses resulted for very little ground captured.

On October 1, the 2nd and 3rd Canadian Divisions, including many battalions that had already been in action, made their first assault on Regina Trench from the obliterated Hessian Trench. Their jump-off positions ran 100 metres north of you in an east-westerly direction, from the row of pylons in the east, to 600 metres to your left. On the far right of the line were the 22nd, 25th and 24th Battalions.

The 24th Battalion attacked 100 metres due north of your position. To the left were the 5th and 4th Canadian Mounted Rifles. The objective, Regina Trench, was 500 metres north. Zero hour was 3:15 p.m.

The attack ran into uncut barbed wire across the front and, unable to pass through rapidly, the Canadian troops were mowed down by the German machine guns. On the left, one company of the 4th Canadian Mounted Rifles reached Regina Trench but was later killed to a man (see Stump Road Cemetery). The attack to the west met the same uncut wire, with similar results. Small parties made it through the wire into the trench, only to be overwhelmed by superior numbers of Germans or forced to evacuate their hard-won positions.

The final tally at the end of the day was the capture of Kenora Trench, where the 24th and 25th Battalions set up trench blocks. The rest of the attack had failed and they paid dearly for inadequate artillery preparation and hurried attacks by battalions depleted by heavy casualties. All this took place along the undulating hills that appear so calm today.

The later attacks of October 8/9, October 21, October 25 and November 1916 on Regina Trench took place east of where you stand. See *Point 7.*

At this point you may wish to visit the cemetery. Return to Courcelette, turn left and go straight through the village. The road then veers to the right. Continue until the road ends and turn left toward Pys or Miraumont. Drive by the village cemetery. After 300 metres you see the quarry and a rough dirt track on your right. If the road is good, follow it for approximately one kilometre. This is Death Valley.

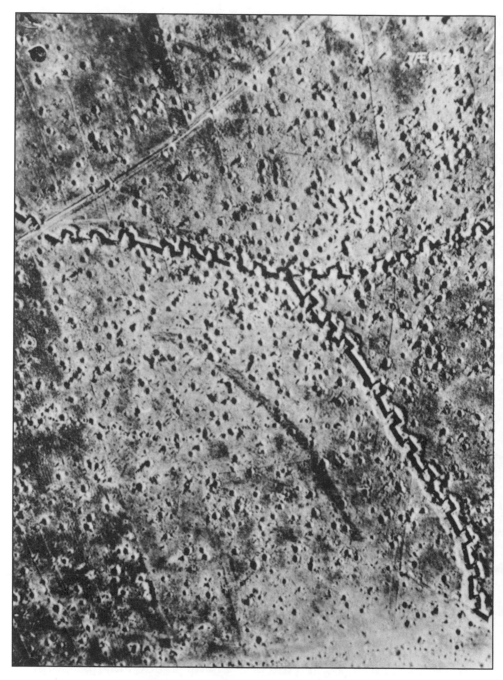

Junction of Regina and Kenora Trenches

(PUBLIC ARCHIVES OF CANADA PAC 14151)

Point 6: Death Valley

The sunken road you have been following, known then as Gun Pit Alley, was captured by the 20th Battalion on September 15. The fighting along the road to the north and to the east was heavy until September 28, when the Germans withdrew to the Regina Trench 1.5 kilometres north of the village. Major actions were fought east of the road on September 22 by the 1st Battalion (Western Ontario) and on September 26/27 by the 28th and 29th Battalions.

One kilometre down the former Dyke Road (Death Valley), you are between The Practice Trenches. These were, as the name suggests, for practice by the Germans before the Great Somme Offensive. They also provided a strong defensive position until they were abandoned on September 28/29. The Germans in this sector were reliant on their main trench position of Regina Trench and, further to the east, a main system running from Le Sars north to Pys.

The Canadians moved into the vacated positions and set up defences by interconnecting shell holes and small trenches. Destremont Farm, the farm southeast of you on the main Albert-Bapaume road, was still held by the Germans. This was the jump-off position before the second main attack on Regina Trench October 8, 1916.

Death Valley, a crescent-shaped gully that provided some protection for troops moving up the line through Courcelette, continues in a northeasterly direction to the Le Sars-Pys road north of Le Sars. As its name implies, it probably did not offer enough protection.

On the rise, among the trees on the north side of the valley, there is still evidence of the war. Shell craters still scar the surface of the embankments and much military ordnance, rusted after 80 years, lies in the grass. The fields in this area, and in the Somme overall, contain a lot of dangerous ordnance, live shells, rusted shell fragments, shrapnel balls and bullets. It does not take much searching to find evidence of the Great War around Courcelette.

Return to Gun Pit Road, turn right on the East Miraumont Road, continue as far as Adanac Cemetery, about 1.5 kilometres north along the road. Stop the car.

Point 7: The capture of Regina and Desire Trenches, November 1916

To the south of the cemetery is the village of Courcelette. The scrubby trees east of the village mark Death Valley and Le Sars and Destremont Farm are further east.

Regina Trench crossed the main East Miraumont Road 200 metres south of the cemetery and continued in an easterly direction for 1.8 kilometres. Near the Le Sars-Pys road, it intersected with other German trenches to form what was known as the Quadrilateral.

The western extension of the trench crossed the fields toward Thiepval, following each dip and undulation of the rolling fields.

Regina Trench Cemetery is 1.4 kilometres from Adanac. The western extension passed 100 metres north of that cemetery and continued for 2.2 kilometres in a westerly direction to the German defensive positions on the Thiepval Ridge.

It was first assaulted by the Canadians, unsuccessfully, on October 1. This time they would attack from near Le Sars to *Point 5*, northwest of Courcelette, a distance of three kilometres. They would jump off from the ruins of Hessian Trench, the advanced positions in Kenora Trench and east of where you stand, from Death Valley. They had between 200 and 500 metres to cover. The attack was launched at 4:50 a.m. on October 8.

The 3rd, 4th, 13th and 16th Battalions, all elements of the 1st Canadian Division, attacked east from the Pys-Courcelette road to Destremont Farm. The 3rd Division, i.e., the 49th Battalion, Royal Canadian Regiment, 43rd and 58th Battalions attacked Regina Trench from the Pys-Courcelette road westwards. Their objective was to capture and hold the trench.

As with the attack of October 1, there was insufficient artillery preparation, there was uncut wire in many places and the trench was undamaged. The left attack (or the west) immediately ran into trouble with the uncut wire. On the far left, the 49th Battalion lost its direction and failed to reach Regina Trench. The Royal Canadian Regiment broke through, captured their portion of the trench and pushed forward 200 metres north. Unfortunately the 43rd and 58th Battalions, the latter attacking 600 metres due south of where you stand, ran into uncut wire and were smashed by the German machine guns.

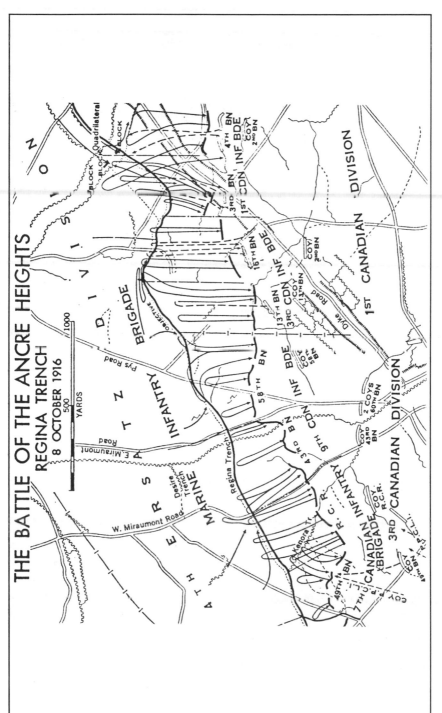

THE BATTLE OF THE ANCRE HEIGHTS
REGINA TRENCH
8 OCTOBER 1916

The Second Assault on Regina Trench

(DEPARTMENT OF NATIONAL DEFENSE)

View of Courcelette from Adanac Cemetery

(PHOTO N. CHRISTIE)

"The Road to Death", Sunken Road Beyond Courcelette

(PUBLIC ARCHIVES OF CANADA PA 712)

Unable to maintain their success, the Royal Canadian Regiment was forced by German counterattacks to withdraw and, like other Canadians who managed to reach Regina Trench, were killed or captured. Five hundred metres east of Adanac cemetery, the 13th Black Watch was stopped by barbed wire. The 16th Battalion was also held up and trapped in front of the trench. The troops suffered severely during one of the most courageous actions of the war.

His officer killed, Piper James Richardson of the 16th Battalion stood up and, refusing to heed the danger, strode along the wire in the face of heavy machine-gun fire playing his bagpipes.

Surprisingly, he wasn't killed and he set such an example for his comrades that the soldiers of the 16th surged forward to capture their portion of Regina Trench. This took place 800 metres southeast of the cemetery.

The 3rd and 4th Battalions also entered Regina Trench, killed the German garrison with bombs and bullets and linked up with the 16th. It was the most successful operation of the day.

However good this appeared, German counterattacks and an inability to reinforce the Canadians in Regina Trench made the position untenable and on October 9, all positions in the trench were evacuated and the Canadians returned to their trenches. Those unable to return were killed or captured.

The 16th Battalion suffered 138 dead, 179 wounded and 26 taken prisoner. One of the dead was Piper James Richardson, who was posthumously awarded the Victoria Cross for his bravery.[5] For the 16th, the battles of the Somme had provided two of their worst three casualty lists of the war. The Canadian Corps were exhausted but it had entered the Somme battle for the last time.

The initial successes of September 15 seemed a long way off and, since that day, it had fought hard, suffered greatly and obtained little. Unfortunately, the Somme had not seen the end of the Canadians.

---

[5] James Richardson was born in Bellshill, Scotland on November 25, 1985.

The 4th Canadian Infantry Division arrived in Flanders in August 1916 and now it was coming south to the Somme to capture Regina Trench. On October 21, battalions of the 4th Division attacked Regina Trench from the East Miraumont Road to a line 500 metres east of the Pys road. The 102nd Battalion attacked north into the triangle created by the fork in the East Miraumont and Pys roads and Regina Trench. East of the Pys road, the 87th Battalion also attacked and was in the trench within 15 minutes. This time the artillery had done its job. The 102nd Battalion advanced up the East Miraumont Road to where you now stand, successfully blocked the ends of the trench and held it. It seemed easy.

On October 25, under severe ground and weather conditions, the 44th Battalion attacked Regina Trench 700 metres east of Adanac Cemetery. The wire was uncut, the artillery not heavy enough to eliminate the German garrison, and rain, mud and cold became the enemy. Isolated, the 44th suffered 200 dead, wounded and missing. Not one man reached Regina Trench. For its first real action of the war, the 44th had suffered bravely and accomplished nothing.

Although the British High Command persisted with the Somme Offensive, the futility of the battle was no longer in doubt to the troops.

On November 11, the 4th Division was again ordered to attack Regina Trench, this time 700 metres east of Adanac Cemetery. The victims for this phase were the 46th and 47th Battalions. As on October 21, the attack took place at midnight (November 10/11). Artillery accomplished its task, the garrison was eliminated and Regina Trench was in Canadian hands. It had taken 41 days to advance 500 metres along a 3.7 kilometre front.

At times, as you walk or drive through this area, you can feel the futility of the Battle of the Somme — lives lost to capture a trench only to witness the digging of another by the Germans, again and again and again.

On November 18, the 4th Division was ordered to capture Desire Trench, a trench running east-west across the Miraumont roads 200 metres north of the cemetery. The West Miraumont Road runs by the power pylons west of Adanac Cemetery. The

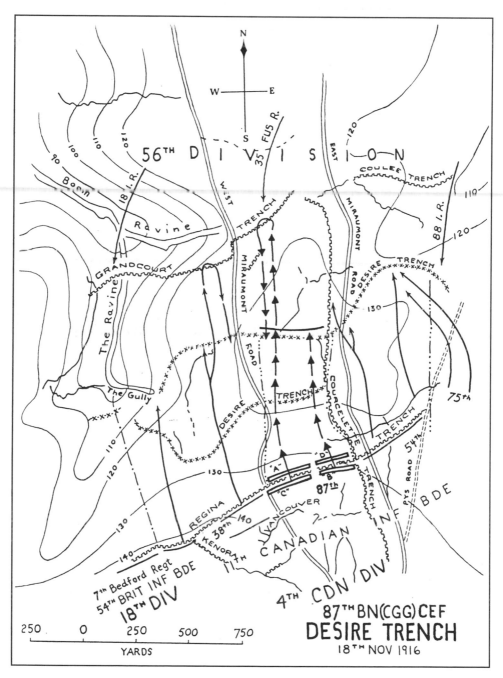

The Capture of Desire Trench

(CANADIAN GRENADIER GUARDS)

VICTOR EDWARD TUXFORD

Victor Edward Tuxford was born in Limehouse, London, England on February 24, 1886. He was the son of Richard Tuxford. We do not know specifically what became of the Tuxford family, but Victor was taken in by the Dr. Barnardo's Homes at the age of 10.

The Barnardo's Homes were established in 1870 by Dr. Thomas John Barnardo, whose idea was to remove orphaned, destitute and abandoned children from the streets of the inner cities of England and give them the security and religious training to redeem what would probably have become hopeless lives.

Barnardo developed links with the Canadian authorities and despatched his first children to Canada in the 1870s. "The Home Children," which included not only children from Barnardo's program but also children of other like-minded British programs, were sent abroad to work on Canadian farms. More than 30,000 Barnardo children landed in Canada over the next 50 years or so. The reception they received varied but, sadly, many were used as cheap labor.

One of those sent was Victor Tuxford. He arrived in Canada in 1903 and worked as a rug cutter in Milton, Ontario.

As a member of the 20th Halton Rifles Militia, he was part of the first contingent of Canadians to sail for England in October 1914. Suffering from shell shock after the Second Battle of Ypres in April 1915, Tuxford was evacuated to England. He returned to his unit in September 1916 and was listed as missing after the attack of Regina Trench October 8/9, 1916. His body was found in 1919 and buried in Adanac Cemetery, Plot 6, Row A, Grave 20. He was 30 when he died.

During the war, 6,211 Barnardo boys served with the Canadian Expeditionary Force. Five hundred and fourteen died.

Canadians jumped off from an east-west line 500 metres west of Adanac Cemetery to a point 600 metres east of it. Regina Trench was by now so damaged it could offer little protection to its Canadian conquerors.

The 38th, 87th, 54th, 75th and 50th Battalions attacked from west to east along a front of two kilometres. The attack went well, except that the British flank was held up. They captured Desire Trench and its support trench and entered Grandcourt Trench, 400 metres distant. However, unsupported, the men were forced to withdraw.

The last battle of the Somme was over. November 18 cost the Canadians 1,250 killed, wounded and missing.

Before you leave the cemetery look south and southwest to Courcelette and Pozières where the Canadians first attacked on September 15, 1916. For a cost of more than 8,000 dead, they advanced only this distance. Thousands of German, Canadian, Australian and British dead were buried in the fields before you, in marked and unmarked graves, in shell holes, collapsed dugouts or obliterated trenches.

From 1919 to 1921, these battlefields were cleared but thousands of bodies were still being found in the 1930s. Between 1931 and 1935, more than 7,000 British, Canadian, Australian, New Zealand and South African bodies were found on the Somme battlefields. What had they gained?

Drive the 2.3 kilometres back to the Albert-Bapaume road. Turn left toward Le Sars and Bapaume. You will arrive in Le Sars after 2.6 kilometres. Turn left on the D74 to Pys, drive 1.2 kilometres past a quarry on your right and down a hill. Turn left on the paved farm road and follow it for 700 metres until you come to a livestock shelter on the right. Stop.

Point 8: The Quadrilateral — the right flank, October to November 1916

You are standing on a slight ridge overlooking the main junction of the German trenches. Directly northeast of here was the infamous position of the Quadrilateral. The village of Le Sars is visible to the east. The large farm 750 metres south of the village was Destremont Farm, today called Le Chateau Farm. The view south shows the treetops of Death Valley and Courcelette. Adanac Cemetery is 1.2 kilometres to the west. Regina Trench ran 200

D'ARCY REIN WADSWORTH
LIEUTENANT, *75th Battalion, C.E.F.*

WILLIAM J. J. MARTIN
PRIVATE, *73rd Battalion, C.E.F.*

Was born in Toronto, Ontario, in October, 1893. He was educated at St. Alban's School, at Ridley College, St. Catharines, and at Upper Canada College, Toronto. In 1910 he entered the service of the Bank of Montreal. He enlisted in May, 1915, as a Private in the 23rd Pioneers Battalion and went overseas with his unit in June, 1916. After a brief period of training in England, he was sent to France in August with a reinforcement draft for the 75th Battalion, Canadian Infantry. During the fighting on the Somme he was detailed to take a course in bombing, and on his return to his battalion after successfully completing his course he was appointed Bombing Officer of his company. On the morning of October 17th, 1916, while giving instruction, he was severely wounded by the premature explosion of a bomb. He died on the following day from his wounds.

Was born in Quebec City, Quebec, in December, 1897. He received his education at the Commercial Academy in his native city. After leaving school he entered the service of the Bank of Montreal, in May, 1914, and was employed in Quebec and later in Granby. He enlisted in Montreal in October, 1915, as a Private in the 73rd Battalion, Royal Highlanders of Canada, and went overseas with his regiment in March, 1916. After a few weeks training in England he proceeded to France with his unit in the following summer. His battalion was at once ordered to the Somme, where intense fighting was in progress. He had been in the line but a few weeks when he was severely wounded by enemy fire while in action with his unit on the morning of November 2nd, 1916. He died from his wounds a few hours later in No. 4 Casualty Clearing Station.

metres south of the cemetery, twisted across the fields along the shallow contours and finally curved at the Quadrilateral passing in front of you

Depending on the season, the chalk spoil left by the digging of the trenches is still evident, even after 80 years. In the field in front of you and running to the Quadrilateral, the chalk still discolors the surface and the ground is softer.

Tramp metal, lead shrapnel balls, copper driving bands, brass fuse caps, cartridges and bullets are still common finds in this area. The author found more than 1,000 shrapnel balls during a two-hour search around Regina Trench. Canadian buttons, bayonets, cartridge clips and "live" grenades and shells also surface regularly. Please remember these are privately-owned fields and permission must be obtained before entering them.

This position offers the best view of the eastern battlefield of October to November 1916. On October 8, the 16th Battalion left its position in Death Valley and attacked across the field toward Regina Trench. Once it crossed the rise, the German machine guns opened fire. The 16th looked for openings in the barbed wire, but few appeared. This was when Piper Richardson piped them onwards and it was across those same fields that the 16th retreated. (The same view applies for the successful operation by the 4th Canadian Division on October 21.)

The extreme right flank attack of October 8 involved the successful attack of the 3rd and 4th Battalions who also jumped off out of Death Valley. They captured the German trenches and the Quadrilateral but were forced to retreat due to the failure of the other battalions.

Amid this tranquil rolling countryside, it is hard to imagine the death and destruction that took place in these fields. Yet the evidence that rises through the soil year after year gives the story away.

Return to Le Sars. Turn left on the Albert-Bapaume road and left again to Arras. Arras is 22 kilometres from Bapaume. (Albert is worth a visit.)

GERALD FREDERICK KENNEDY

CORPORAL, *87th Battalion, C.E.F.*

Was born in Montreal on September 28th, 1896. After receiving his education at the Mount Royal and the Technical High Schools in his native city, he entered the service of the Bank of Montreal in July, 1912. He enlisted in Montreal in September, 1915, as a Private in the 87th Battalion, Canadian Grenadier Guards. While training at St. Johns, Quebec, some weeks later, he was promoted to Corporal. He arrived in France with his unit in 1916 during the period of severe fighting on the Somme. Because of his reliability and efficiency he was detailed for duty with the scouts section of his brigade, with which he served until his death. He was instantly killed by enemy fire while carrying out a task of danger and daring on October 21st, 1916, during the intense attack for the taking of Regina Trench on the Somme. He was buried where he fell.

PHILIP KEITH BEALL

LANCE-CORPORAL, *72nd Battalion, C.E.F.*

Was born in Burbage, England, in 1890. He received his education at the Bedford School where he was noted as an athlete. Before he entered the service of the Bank of British North America in London, England, he was employed for over three years in the Capital and Counties Bank Limited. He was transferred to Canada in 1913. He enlisted in Vancouver, B.C., in March, 1916, as a Private in the 72nd Battalion, Seaforth Highlanders of Canada, and reached France in August, 1916. He was appointed Lance-Corporal and detailed for duty with the bombing section of his battalion, with which he served continuously during the autumn months. On November 23rd, 1916, he was instantly killed by enemy fire while leading his company bombers in an attack on an enemy trench. Before his death he had been recommended for a commission.

(PUBLIC ARCHIVES OF CANADA PA 868)

The Dead on the Field of Battle

CLEARING THE BATTLEFIELDS

The numbers are shocking. The remains of more than 600,000 Commonwealth servicemen lie buried in some 3,500 cemeteries carved into the rolling hills and farmers' fields of northern France and Belgium.

Landscaped and constructed during the 1920s by the Imperial War Graves Commission (now the Commonwealth War Graves Commission), these cemeteries have frozen the history of the First World War.

The principles of the IWGC, established in 1917 to maintain the cemeteries and record the Commonwealth[6] dead of the Great War (and later the Second World War), were threefold:

1) The name of each serviceman who died in the war or during the immediate postwar would be commemorated on a headstone or engraved on a battlefield memorial.

2) All would receive universal treatment in death.

3) No bodies would be repatriated. All would remain in the country where they died.

The repatriation restriction and the acquisition of the land where the cemeteries originally stood have preserved for perpetuity the legacy left by the hundreds of thousands who sacrificed their lives in foreign lands.

Cemetery Categories

The types of cemeteries fall into three main categories:

1) *Hospital Centre Cemeteries* are near main hospital centres or casualty clearing stations. All burials are in chronological order and few graves are unidentified. The officers usually have a separate burial plot, as do Hindus, Moslems and Buddhists. Serviceman of the Jewish faith are usually buried in the Christian plots but there are exceptions. In Étaples, a plot for black soldiers (generally of the British West Indies Regiment) includes one Canadian.

2) *Regimental or Front-Line Cemeteries* are cemeteries near the front lines for quick burial of soldiers killed at the front (trench

---

[6] The term Commonwealth applies to countries of the old British Empire, namely Australia, New Zealand, India, Pakistan, Canada, South Africa, Britain and other British colonies or protectorates.

wastage) or small battlefield cemeteries set up by Divisional or Corps Burial Officers immediately after a battle. Often the layout and rows are irregular.

3) *Battlefield Clearance Cemeteries* were usually small cemeteries greatly expanded after the war by the concentration of remains brought in from surrounding battlefields. They always contain a very high proportion of unidentified graves and the layout of the rows is regular and often symmetric.

Burying the Dead

During the immediate postwar period, the victors faced hundreds of square miles of devastated land, a seemingly infinite amount of war material and munitions and the thousands of isolated graves, both marked and unmarked, scattered throughout the battlefields.

During the war the dead were often buried by their comrades in small regimental cemeteries directly behind the front lines or in cemeteries created near hospitals or Casualty Clearing Stations For those who fell in the heat of battle, or on territory lost to the Germans, buried by explosions or fallen in areas under constant fire, burial was a rare occurrence. Burial parties made nighttime expeditions into the front line or into No Man's Land where they would place the dead in a shell hole and cover them quickly with a cursory layer of earth. It was a nasty, unpopular and dangerous task and those assigned to the duty would complete it as quickly as possible. The dead were dead.

Lists of missing, often presumed dead, from the war ran into the hundreds of thousands. In France and Belgium alone, more than 300,000 are missing or have no known grave.

Throughout the war the Directorate of Grave Registrations and Enquiries (DGRE) in association with Grave Registration Units (GRU) registered each grave, where possible, and established a system to receive all burial reports from Divisional Burial Officers or chaplains. A master list was kept in London. When the war ended, these records were used to establish a procedure for the battlefield clearances of 1919 through 1921.

The Clearers

After the armistice, Royal Engineer Labor Companies were organized to systematically clear the individual battlefields. The procedures and responsibilities developed for the clearances are outlined below:

1) **The survey officer** laid out the area to be searched. He was responsible for instructing the Labor Companies or Exhumation Parties where to conduct the searches and where reburial should take place.

   Land for the permanent war cemeteries was acquired by the DGRE via international agreements with the host countries. Normally, the survey officer selected 500-yard squares to be searched and marked the corners with flags. Existing small battlefield cemeteries within the square were marked with blue flags if they contained more than 40 burials and yellow flags if less than 40. These cemeteries were left untouched until specific orders were received to concentrate the burials to a permanent cemetery.

   The survey officer also indicated to the officer commanding the exhumations the anticipated number of remains to be found in the area to be searched. This estimate was based on the burial records of the DGRE.

2) **The Army Burial Officer** was in charge of the exhumations. It was his responsibility to ensure the procedures for exhumation were correctly followed and the correct paperwork completed. This responsibility ended when the bodies arrived at the permanent war cemetery.

3) **The Registration Officer** was responsible for the digging parties working inside the permanent war cemeteries. He sanctioned the digging of new graves, the erection of suitable crosses and the completion of the necessary paperwork, correct and in triplicate.

The Exhumation Companies

The principal and most disagreeable task fell to the men of the exhumation companies. Their objective was not only to clear the battlefields for sanitary reasons but to identify the remains which had often been left in shell holes for more than six years!

It was essential, therefore, that the area be searched carefully and systematically. The men were assured their work was vital in determining the fate of the large number of men who, in 1919, 1920 and 1921, were still listed as missing. If the work was done carefully, many could be found and identified.

The exhumation company was organized into squads of 32 men and subdivided into squads of four. Each squad was supplied with a 500-square-yard map (already surveyed and designated by the Survey Officer), two pairs of rubber gloves, two shovels, stakes to mark the locations of graves found, canvas and rope to tie up remains, stretchers, cresol (a poisonous colorless isomeric phenol) and wire cutters.

The officer in charge had a map of the area (1:20,000 scale), labels to attach to the bodies, ration bags for recovered personal effects and a notebook. All remains, whether Allied or German, were to be removed from the battlefield and concentrated into a permanent war cemetery.

The search would start in the 500-yard square. The men were instructed not to bunch and to span the ground slowly, placing a stake where remains were found. After a thorough search, they would return to each stake and exhume the remains. When the graves were unmarked, experience was the only method of knowing where to dig. However, characteristic signs were as follows:

i) rifles or stakes protruding from the ground, bearing helmets or equipment;

ii) partial remains or equipment on the surface or protruding from the ground;

iii) rat holes — often small bones or pieces of equipment will be brought to the surface by the rats;

iv) discoloration of grass, earth or water — grass was often a vivid bluish-green with broader blades where bodies were buried, while earth and water turned a greenish-black or grey color;

Generally, many more remains than DGRE documents indicated were found. Once the area had been searched, they would commence the task of exhumation.

A Nauseating Experience

In 1919, this task was most unpleasant as much of the corpse remained and were quite repulsive to touch. Identifying corpses whose identification discs had been driven into the flesh by a projectile was also a considerable problem. By 1921 decomposition made the task less disagreeable.

The exhumation squad would dig gently around the stake (in case more than one body was buried) and place the body or bodies on cresol-soaked canvas. For identification purposes, a careful examination of pockets, the neck, wrists and braces (places where soldiers often kept their identification tags) was required.

All personal effects would be placed in a ration bag. The body would be wrapped in the canvas and tied. The ration bag and tag (listing map reference, name, unit, list of effects found, etc. and cemetery to be reburied) would be attached to the canvas. Only the officer-in-charge was permitted to complete this label.

He would also indicate on the tag whether a committal service was necessary, depending on whether he believed the body had previously been properly committed. Remains were then placed on a transport wagon or in a field ambulance and taken to a permanent war cemetery, accompanied by the original cross if any.

Once the body had been removed from the grave, any equipment not required for identification was returned to the grave, the ground treated with cresol and the grave filled. If more than one body was found in a grave the remains were kept together so they could be reburied together in a permanent cemetery. This was done to allow future identification should additional records shed light on the burials.

The Flyers

The local people who had fled their homes and farms in the battle-torn areas of France and Belgium returned quickly after the war. During reconstruction of the villages, remains found were recovered by the exhumation company's "Flying Squads." The transport proceeded to a designated permanent cemetery where the registration officer and the cemetery party took control.

At the Permanent War Cemetery

The party at the permanent war cemetery comprised the registration officer, a chaplain, a digging party of the 20 men and a sanitary man. The cemetery was laid out in advance, subdivided into plots and rows and a 40-foot trench, 4.5 feet deep, hollowed out. When the transport arrived, the remains were interred in pre-selected locations and any original crosses were placed at the head of the graves. If there was no cross, a GRU cross with stamped aluminum identification strip was erected.

The Effects Branch

At this point the personal effects were reexamined for identification and then forwarded to the Effects Branch at the Base. The graves were filled and the chaplain read the burial service over the remains (if necessary). If German prisoner-of-war labor was used for digging the graves, the POWS were removed from the cemetery during the committal service. The stretchers were washed with cresol and returned to the exhumation parties. During working hours visitors were not admitted to the cemetery.

Between 1919 and 1921, 200,000 concentrations took place in France and Belgium. Less than half of those exhumed were identified.

Completion

Throughout the 1920s, the permanent war cemeteries you see today were constructed and landscaped. The burial mounds were leveled and headstones replaced the wooden crosses.

Nearly eight decades on, the maintenance of these war graves is big business! The operating budget for the Commonwealth War Graves Commission, which is based in England and has offices in France, Belgium and Italy, is approximately $60,000,000 (1995). Canada is responsible for 10 per cent of this.

The grave of a serviceman can be traced through the CWGC offices. "Cemetery overprint" Michelin maps can also be obtained from its offices in Maidenhead, England; Arras, France; Yprès, Belgium; and Rome, Italy. Map Numbers 51, 52 and 53 cover the Western Front. Map 53 covers the Somme (1:200,000).

CEMETERIES AND MEMORIALS

The remains of 5,000 Canadians killed in the Battle of the Somme were never identified or found. Their bones were scattered in ensuing battles or still lie buried, lost somewhere in the chalky farmlands of the Somme. Others were buried as unknown Canadian soldiers. Roughly 60 per cent of the Canadians killed in the Battle of the Somme have no known grave.[7]

The ferocious fighting in a compact area and the massive bombardments contributed to this large percentage of missing. Some families received no more news about their lost sons, husbands and brothers than "Missing, presumed dead." These men apparently vanished without a trace, obliterated by the machinery of war.

During the Great War a general rule applied: A decisive win of a battle that drove the enemy back resulted in 90 per cent of the dead receiving a known and honored burial. A loss, or continuous battle over the same positions, meant few honored burials.

Such was the case with the Battle of the Somme and throughout the First World War. There are more than 425,000 identified burials in France and Belgium and 318,000 names of soldiers with no identified grave. This statistic indicates that 43 per cent of the 743,000 Commonwealth soldiers who died in France and Flanders were missing or had graves lost!

Also consider that the dual identification disc system was not introduced until late in 1916. The one aluminum tag or bracelet worn by the soldiers was normally removed from the body for identification at the time of death. This meant no identification would be available when the body was later located. Throughout the 1920s and 1930s, thousands of remains were found in isolated graves on the Somme. In 1934, 642 graves were found. In 1935, a further 738 were unearthed.

---

[7] In France the names of 220,000 Commonwealth soldiers with no known grave are engraved on the memorials to the missing. In the cemeteries there are only 110,000 graves of unidentified soldiers. This leaves 110,000 soldiers unaccounted for. Their remains still rest in the soil of France.

The Canadians killed on the Somme who do not have a known grave are commemorated by name on the Vimy Memorial. The rest are buried in one of 410 war cemeteries on the Somme. Principal cemeteries are listed below.

THE VIMY MEMORIAL

The Vimy Memorial, eight kilometres north of Arras off the road to Bethune, is Canada's National Memorial erected by the people of Canada to commemorate the Canadian sacrifice in the Great War. It also commemorates 11,285 Canadian soldiers who died in France and have a no known graves. The 6,983 who died in Belgium and have no known graves are commemorated on the Menin Gate Memorial. The two memorials commemorate a total of 18,268 Canadians, or 30 per cent of all the Canadians who fell in France and Flanders during the Great War.

COURCELETTE BRITISH CEMETERY

One kilometre west of the village of Courcelette, this cemetery was enlarged by battlefield clearances after the war. It now contains the graves of 1,956 Commonwealth soldiers including 783 Canadians, 384 of them unidentified. Most of the Canadian soldiers buried here were killed west of the village on September 15, 1916, in later battles September 16 to 20, during the assault on Hessian Trench September 26 and in the first assault on Regina Trench October 1.

Among those commemorated here is Lieutenant J. C. Mewburn, son of the Minister of Militia and Defense, Major General S. C. Mewburn of Hamilton. He was killed at Courcelette on September 15, 1916.

REGINA TRENCH CEMETERY

Regina Trench cemetery is one kilometre northwest of Courcelette. The original part of the cemetery (Plot 2, Rows A through D) was made in 1916 and 1917 and then enlarged after the war by battlefield clearances. It now contains 2,265 Commonwealth burials including 564 Canadians, of whom 192 are unknown.

The Canadians buried here are predominantly those killed on the left flank of the Canadian assaults against Regina Trench on October 1 and October 8 and on Desire Trench November 18, 1916.

View of Courcelette British Cemetery from just west of the village.

(PHOTO N. CHRISTIE)

Pozières British Cemetery c.1919

ADANAC MILITARY CEMETERY

Found one kilometre northeast of Courcelette, Adanac cemetery was made from battlefield clearances after the war. It contains 3,172 Commonwealth burials, of which 1,071 are Canadian, 510 (48 per cent) unidentified.

The men buried in the cemetery reflect nearly all the units involved in the fighting of September 15, local fighting east of Courcelette, the second assault on Regina Trench, October 8 and the later attacks of October 25 and November 11 and the capture of Desire Trench on November 18.

Piper James Richardson, VC, of the 16th Canadian Scottish is buried in Plot 3, Row F, Grave 36. A New Zealander Victoria Cross winner, Sergeant S. Forsyth, of the New Zealand Engineers is buried in Plot 1, Row 1, Grave 39.

POZIÈRES BRITISH CEMETERY

Pozières cemetery, just west of the village of Pozières on the main Albert-Bapaume Road, contains the graves of 2,733 Commonwealth soldiers, 218 of them Canadian. Of those, 68 are unknown. After the war, battlefields clearances greatly enlarged the cemetery.

The Canadian burials reflect the fighting around Pozières from September 4 through 9, the attack on Courcelette September 15 and subsequent fighting west of the village.

The grave of Sergeant C. C. Castleton, VC, who won his Victoria Cross posthumously with the Australian Machine Gun Corps at Pozières, is buried in Plot 4, Row L, Grave 43.

The cemetery is also the location for the Pozières Memorial to the Missing, on whose walls are engraved the names of 14,674 British soldiers killed in the German offensive on the Somme in 1918 who have no known grave.

OVILLERS MILITARY CEMETERY

The cemetery is about four kilometres from Albert, west of Ovillers village, directly north of the Albert-Bapaume Road. Battlefield clearances in 1920 enlarged the cemetery. It now contains the graves of 3,183 Commonwealth soldiers including 95 Canadians, of which 68 are unidentified.

The Grave of Private Richardson VC, Adanac Cemetery

(PHOTO N. CHRISTIE)

The bodies of the Canadian soldiers were found on the Courcelette battlefield and reflect the battles throughout September, October and November 1916.

BAPAUME POST MILITARY CEMETERY

The cemetery is on the Albert-Bapaume road, two kilometres east of Albert. It was employed in 1916 and 1917 and enlarged after the war from battlefield clearances. The graves of 409 Commonwealth soldiers, including 64 Canadians (all identified) are located here.

The Canadian burials are predominantly officers whose bodies were recovered from the battlefields and reburied in 1916. Among them is Lieutenant Henry Scott of the 87th Grenadiers Guards of Montreal, killed at Regina Trench on October 21, 1916. He was the son of Canon Frederick Scott, Padre of the 1st Canadian Division.

Canon Scott was famous throughout the war for his character and poetry. After the war he wrote the famous "Great War" book, *The Great War as I Saw It* (1928).

Also buried in the cemetery are the commanding officers of the 20th and 23th Battalions of the Northumberland Fusiliers, killed during a disastrous attack at Ovillers on July 1, 1916. Lieutenant Colonel C. Sillery and W. Lyle are buried in Plot 1, Row G, Graves 2 and 1 respectively.

ALBERT COMMUNAL CEMETERY EXTENSION

This cemetery is on the southeast side of the town. It was used by fighting units and ambulances from 1915 to 1918. It contains the graves of 863 graves of which 202 (all identified) are Canadian.

Many of the Canadians were officers killed in the battle near Courcelette and brought back to Albert for an honored burial. Among those buried here are the commanding officers of the 13th and 43rd Battalions and the 6th Canadian Field Ambulance.

The cemetery reflects the high cost of senior officers from the 13th Battalion killed when a shell struck their dugout headquarters at Courcelette on September 26, 1916: Lieutenant Colonel Victor Buchanan, DSO, buried in Plot 1, Row P, Grave 24; Major Wilfred Peterman, buried in Plot 1, Row P, Grave 27; and Captain Carleton Green, buried in Plot 1, Row P, Grave 26.

The Grave of Captain H. H. Scott

(PHOTO N. CHRISTIE)

Postcard Circa 1919, Albert Communal Cemetery

Their bodies were removed and brought back for burial in Albert. Canon F. G. Scott officiated at the funeral and read the burial service over the graves. A rifle salute was given and the Last Post was sounded over the graves.

Lieutenant Colonel Robert Thomson, commander of the 43rd Battalion died of wounds received at Regina Trench October 8, 1916. He is buried in Plot 1, Row P, Grave 1. Lieutenant Colonel Roland Campbell, commander of the 6th Canadian Field Ambulance, was killed September 16, 1916 near Courcelette and is buried in Plot 1, Row N, Grave 4.

SUNKEN ROAD CEMETERY, CONTALMAISON

North of Contalmaison on the road to Pozières, this cemetery was used by fighting units. It contains the graves of 214 Commonwealth soldiers, including 148 Canadians. One is unidentified.

2ND CANADIAN CEMETERY, SUNKEN ROAD CONTALMAISON

Located across the road from Sunken Road Cemetery, this cemetery was used exclusively by the 2nd Battalion throughout the Somme Battles and contains 44 identified graves.

Grave of Lieutenant Colonel V. C. Buchanan, DSO

(PHOTO N. CHRISTIE)

STUMP ROAD CEMETERY, GRANDCOURT

The cemetery is found south of Grandcourt on the road to Poziéres. It was made by battlefield clearances in 1917 and contains the graves of 263 Commonwealth soldiers, including 24 Canadians, four of them unidentified.

They are all members of the 2nd and 4th Battalions of the Canadian Mounted Rifles, killed when a company of the 4th Canadian Mounted Rifles broke through at Regina Trench on October 1, 1916. They were cut off and annihilated by German counterattacks. This site gives an excellent view of the Somme Battlefield.

THE HOSPITAL CENTRES

The wounded were evacuated to medical stations at Puchevillers, Contay and Warloy-Baillon and, later, to Rouen and Etaples. Many of those wounded rest in cemeteries in those villages.

CONTAY BRITISH CEMETERY

This beautiful cemetery is located south of the village of Contay, 10 kilometres west of Albert. It was set up predominantly by Casualty Clearing Stations in 1916. It contains 1,133 Commonwealth burials, including 414 Canadians (all identified). Typical of a hospital centre, all burials are in chronological order.

WARLOY-BAILLON COMMUNAL CEMETERY EXTENSION

The cemetery is located east of Warloy-Baillon village, 10 kilometres northwest of Albert, five kilometres from Contay. It contains the graves of 1,330 Commonwealth soldiers, including 152 Canadians (all identified). It is a typical hospital centre cemetery.

Warloy was often used for the more seriously wounded, those with head or femur wounds. Contay accommodated the other wounded.

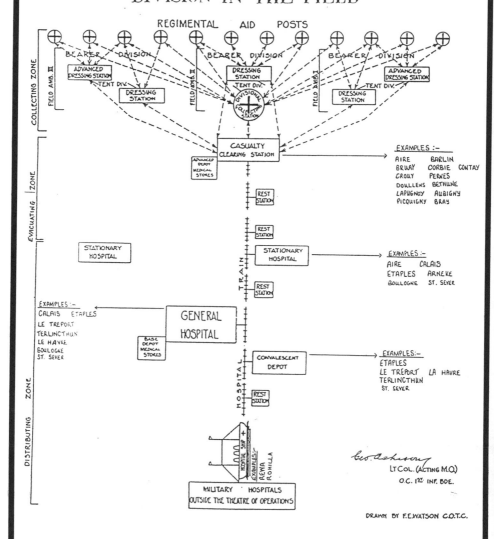

CHART OF THE MEDICAL SERVICE OF A DIVISION IN THE FIELD

PUCHEVILLERS BRITISH CEMETERY

West of the village of Puchevillers and 20 kilometres southwest of Albert, Puchevillers cemetery was used by Casualty Clearing Stations from 1916 to 1918. It contains 1,763 Commonwealth graves, including 214 Canadians (two unidentified).

The Canadians buried here were those mortally wounded in the battle of Poziéres and Courcelette in September 1916.

ETAPLES MILITARY CEMETERY

Etaples cemetery is on the coastal road between Boulogne and Le Touquet, three kilometres north of Etaples. It was used throughout the war and contains 10,729 Commonwealth soldiers, including 1,123 Canadians. This cemetery reflects the Canadian losses in the major actions of Mount Sorrel, the Somme, Vimy, Passchendaele and the Advance to Victory.

Etaples was the major depot base for the British army on the Western Front and was the location of the infamous Bull Ring and the British mutiny in 1917.

On May 19, 1918, German Gotha bombers bombed the depots and direct hits were received on the No. 1 Canadian General hospital, killing 66, including three nursing sisters. The men killed in the attack are buried in Plots 66, 67 and 68. The nursing sisters are buried in Plot 28.

The Discovery of Remains

The initial searches of 1919 and 1920 failed to recover many dead, due to the depths of the trenches and the severity of the battles. Throughout the 1920s and 1930s, thousands of remains were found and buried in open cemeteries throughout the Somme region and sometimes further afield.

A.I.F. BURIAL GROUND, FLERS

A.I.F. Burial Ground contains 67 Canadians killed in the Somme fighting, whose remains were found between 1925 and 1927. Thirty-eight are unidentified.

Étaples Military Cemetery

(PHOTO N. CHRISTIE)

Postcard Circa 1919, Delville Wood Cemetery

SERRE ROAD CEMETERY, NUMBER 1

Here lie the remains of 121 Canadians killed in the Somme battles whose remains were found in 1923. Eighty-six are unidentified.

SERRE ROAD CEMETERY, NUMBER 2

The remains of 301 Canadians killed in the Somme battles were recovered between 1926 and 1931 and buried here. A hundred and eighty-six are unidentified.

DELVILLE WOOD CEMETERY, LONGUEVAL

This cemetery contains the graves of 29 Canadians killed in the Somme battles and recovered from the battlefields in 1922. Twenty-one are unidentified.

LONDON CEMETERY EXTENSION, HIGH WOOD

The graves of 162 Canadians killed in France whose remains were found between 1934 and 1957 are in this cemetery. The remains were brought in from all over the Western Front, but predominantly from the Somme. In 1936 the remains of Corporal John Marshall Hunt of the 3rd Battalion were found. The body of Hunt, considered missing and presumed dead near Pozières on September 4, 1916, was identified by his silver Queen's South Africa Medal (Boer War) with four clasps, which was found with the remains. He is buried in Plot 7, Row J, Grave 11.

Other cemeteries also contain Canadian Somme casualties, varying in number:

Thiepval Anglo-French Cemetery
Mont Huon Military Cemetery, Le Treport
Suzanne Military Cemetery No. 3
Tincourt New British Cemetery
Warlencourt British Cemetery
Bazentin le Petit Communal Cemetery Extension
Bouzincourt Ridge Cemetery, Albert
Caterpillar Valley Cemetery, Longueval
Cerisy-Gailly Military Cemetery
Dantzig Alley British Cemetery, Mametz

PRIVATE (PIPER) JAMES RICHARDSON, V.C.
Late 16th Batallion

"For most conspicuous bravery and devotion to duty when, prior to attack [October 8th, 1916, at Regina Trench], he obtained permission from his commanding officer to play his company 'over the top.' As the company reached the objective, it was held up by very strong wire, and came under intense fire, which caused heavy casualties and demoralized the formation for the moment. Realizing the situation, Piper Richardson strode up and down outside the wire, playing his pipes with the greatest coolness. The effect was instantaneous. Inspired by his splendid example, the company rushed the wire with such fury and determination that the obstacle was overcome and the position captured. Later, after participating in bombing operations, he was detailed to take back a wounded comrade and prisoners. After proceeding about two hundred yards, Piper Richardson remembered that he had left his pipes behind. Although strongly urged not to do so, he insisted on returning to recover his pipes. He has never been seen since, and death has been presumed accordingly, owing to lapse of time."

Citations for the Victoria Cross
The Somme 1916

PRIVATE JOHN CHIPMAN KERR, V.C.
49th Battalion

"For most conspicuous bravery. During a bombing attack [September 16th 1916, at Courcelette], he was acting as bayonet man, and knowing that bombs were running short, he ran along the parados under very heavy fire until he was in close contact with the enemy, when he opened fire on them at point-blank range and inflicted heavy loss. The enemy, thinking they were surrounded, surrendered, sixty-two prisoners were taken, and two hundred and fifty yards of enemy trench captured.

"Before carrying out this very plucky act, one of Private Kerr's fingers had been blown off by a bomb. Later, with two other men, he escorted back the prisoners under fire, and then returned to report himself for duty before having his wound dressed."

ACTING-CORPORAL LEONARD CLARKE, V.C.
Late 2nd Battalion

"For most conspicuous bravery [September 10th, 1916, near Pozières].

"He was detailed with his section of bombers to clear the continuation of a newly captured trench, and cover the construction of a 'block.' After most of h is party had become casualties, he was building a 'block' when about twenty of the enemy with two officers counter-attacked. He boldly advanced against them emptied his revolver into them and afterwards two enemy rifles, which he picked up in the trench. One of the officers attacked him with the bayonet, wounding him in the leg, but he shot him dead. The enemy ran away, pursued by Corporal Clarke, who shot four more and captured a fifth. Later, he was ordered to the dressing station, but returned next day to duty."

Citations for the Victoria Cross
The Somme 1916

Canadian National Monument at Vimy Ridge

(PHOTO BY N. CHRISTIE)

ALLWARD'S DREAM

The idea for the magnificient Canadian National Monument, which sits majestically on the Vimy Ridge, came to Toronto architect and sculptor Walter S. Allward in a dream.

Overlooking the Douai Plain on the ridge captured by the Canadian Corps on April 9, 1917, the monument commemorates the 60,000 Canadians who gave their lives in the Great War.

Allward's design won the 1921 national memorial competition and work began in France in 1925. The project went slowly as workers had to cope with a warren of tunnels, mine craters, shell holes, trenches and dugouts on the old Vimy battlefield. The massive number of unexploded shells of all calibers and live grenades prevented the use of large earthmoving equipment. Each section of the construction site had to be cleared by pick and shovel and many men were injured.

It took two years to complete the 3.5 kilometre road leading from Thelus to the monument on Hill 145. Before construction of the road began, craters were drained and rammed and more than 26 dugouts filled and concreted over. Evidence of uncharted dugouts appeared when the ground subsided following heavy rains.

Similar work was required to build the foundation of the monument. More than 15,000 tonnes of concrete and steel reinforcing bars were used to build it. Two men were killed in this phase of the operation.

The next step was the construction of the bastion, the symbol of impregnable defense, surmounted by two pylons representing the gate to eternity and the two countries that paid so heavily to capture the ridge.

The final phase was the sculpting of the 20 statues Allward had envisaged. Each represents a virtue, a higher ideal achieved by the sacrifice of the Canadians. Each statue was sculpted in situ, with a special studio constructed for each. Half-sized plaster models were used by the sculptors. Six thousand tonnes of Trau limestone, quarried from the Dalmation coast, was used for the monument.

The memorial was unveiled on July 26, 1936 by King Edward VIII in the presence of thousands of Canadian veterans and war widows who made the pilgrimage to pay homage to their fallen comrades.

On approaching the memorial, the first statues viewed are the reclining man on the right and a woman on the left, the mourners reflecting on the grief felt by many Canadian families. Angels, carved toward the top of the pylons, guard the gate. This is the "back" of the memorial.

At the front of the monument, between the pylons, are two figures representing the spirit of sacrifice and the passing of the torch. They gaze upwards toward the celestial values.

The three statues on the left pylon reflect Truth and Faith, surmounted by Justice. On the right pylons, similarly represented, are Charity and Knowledge, surmounted by Peace. These spiritual figures are chanting the hymn of peace.

The main statue facing the Douai Plain represents the spirit of Canada mourning her fallen sons. This figure is the largest of the 20 statues and was sculpted from a single 30-tonne block of Dalmation limestone.

At the base of the right-hand stairs of the monument is a group of three statues illustrating the breaking of the sword and the defiance and defeat of militarism.

In the centre of the bastion is the tomb of the fallen Canadian soldier, representing all those who died.

The last group of four statues at the base of the left-hand stairs, represents Canada defending the helpless.

Engraved on the walls of the monument are the names of the 11,285 Canadian soldiers who died in France but were denied a known grave by the fortunes of war. They are listed alphabetically and, secondarily, by rank. The graves of more than 100 men have been found since the panels were engraved in the 1930s.

More than 20 sets of brothers, a father and his son and a Count are named on the memorial. Each name has its own sad story. For example, Private Harold Chapman served as a Major with British forces in Gallipoli, was wounded and discharged.

He returned to Canada and reenlisted in Vancouver. He was killed at Hill 70, August 15, 1917.

There is also at least one man listed who did not die. Private McDonald was listed as wounded and missing in 1918. His pension was paid to his widow and the case was closed until 1957 when another wife of Private McDonald reported his death to local authorities. He had married in England for a second time in 1917, deserted in 1918, returned to Canada and lived the last 40 years of his life in British Columbia!

The memorial is surrounded by 100 hectares (250 acres) of the Vimy battleground, a gift in perpetuity from France to Canada. Within the park, trenches have been preserved along the "crater line" and tours of the underground tunnels are available from April to November.

NATIONALITIES

Immigration to Canada between 1880 and 1914 swelled Canada's population to 7.2 million people (1911). The opening up of Western Canada brought in droves of new Canadians, not only from the mother country, but from Russia, Scandinavia, Japan and the United States.

The members of the original Canadian contingent were predominantly British-born, but by the end of the war Canadian-born soldiers made up 52 per cent of total enlistments. As these statistics are based on the country of birth, they do not reflect the fact that many of these men were raised in Canada. Also, consider the different attitudes in those days. Going to Canada, South Africa or Australia was pretty much one and the same thing for a British citizen. It was further than moving to Devonshire but they were all part of the Empire.

The high percentage of British-born soldiers, then, is not surprising. What *is* surprising are the many different nationalities represented by the enlistments.

By country of birth, the statistics are as follows:

	The 1st Contingent (country of birth) 1914	Total enlistments in the CEF 1914-19
Canada	10,880 (30 per cent)	318,705 (52 per cent)
British Isles	23,211 (64 per cent)	228,174 (36 per cent)
Other Countries	2,176 (6 per cent)	72,757 (12 per cent)

This table clearly shows the enthusiasm of recent British immigrants (the second contingent was predominantly British-born as well) and also the enthusiasm of men born in other countries as the war progressed. These men were principally Americans who either immigrated to Canada or crossed the border to participate in the great adventure.

Still, the wide dispersion of nationalities is fascinating. The enthusiasm of those who came from other Empire countries is to be expected: white colonials from New Zealand, Australia, South Africa, Ceylon, India, Newfoundland and the British West Indies. The surprise is in the enlistments from Italy, Switzerland, Belgium (Walloon and Flemand), France, Norway, Sweden, Denmark, Iceland, Greece, Montenegro, Egypt, Russia, Venezuela, Argentina and Mexico, to name a few. They made up 12 per cent of total enlistments.

The white man's Great War also attracted others to join the colors in Canada: the Japanese-Canadians, the Sikhs, Black Canadians, and native Canadians. Though they were considered, by the men who ran the war, to be lesser races and even "ignorant children," in that unmalicious "that is all you can expect of them" racism of the period, still they enlisted and served. German names do crop up on the enlistments, but many German-Austrian Canadians were interned during the war.

Within the statistics of those born in Britain, 69 per cent were English-born, 21 per cent Scottish, eight percent Irish and two per cent Welsh. But they all wanted to belong to a kilted regiment.

CHARLES EDWARD MERRIX

PRIVATE, *28th Battalion, C.E.F.*

THOMAS ALFRED JONES

PRIVATE, *16th Battalion, C.E.F.*

Was born in Shoreham, Sussex, England, in January, 1897. After completing his education in the Municipal Secondary School in Brighton, he came to Canada and entered the service of the Bank of Montreal in Port Arthur in 1912. In April, 1916, he enlisted as a Private in the 94th Battalion, Canadian Infantry, and in the following July he arrived in England with his unit which was subsequently broken up into drafts. After a brief period of training, he went to France in August, 1916, with a reinforcement draft for the 28th Battalion, Canadian Infantry, then in action on the Somme front where severe fighting was in progress. He reached the firing line on September 12th, and three days later, on the early morning of September 15th, 1916, he was instantly killed by enemy fire while advancing with his platoon in the attack at Courcelette.

Was born in Newtown, North Wales, in 1892. He was educated at Dolfar Church School and at Newtown Church School; later he won a scholarship in the Newtown Intermediate School, where in successive years he obtained the Junior and the Senior Certificates of the Central Welsh Board. After completing his education he came to Canada in November, 1910, and entered the service of the Bank of Montreal. In 1916 he enlisted as a Private in the 72nd Battalion, Seaforth Highlanders of Canada, and after some weeks of training he went to France with a reinforcement draft for the Canadian Scottish Battalion then in action on the Somme front. In September, 1916, he was severely wounded by enemy fire during an attack near Courcelette on the Somme. He died from his wounds a few days later, on the 14th of September, 1916.

Many religions were also represented. Jews served Canada with honor. The Star of David is engraved on the headstones of those who died. Sikhs also served with the Army and their unique style headstones are seen in France and Belgium.

Although I have yet to find any Moslem or Buddhist Canadian headstones, I am certain they served, naming as a matter of convenience another more common religion as their faith.

EXECUTIONS

More than 350 British Empire soldiers were executed during the Great War. Twenty-five of these men were Canadian soldiers, all volunteers. Twenty-two were executed for desertion, one for cowardice and two for murder. By contrast, the Australians did not execute a single man during the war.

Military authorities deemed that certain offenses, considered minor in peace time, could not be tolerated on active service. Desertion, which normally resulted in a two-year sentence, could bring the death penalty in wartime.

In theory each man would receive a fair trial with assistance from an experienced defense council. The judgment would be based on the man's record and fighting ability, the extenuating circumstances and previous convictions. Also considered was desertion to avoid a major attack and prevalence of desertion in the soldier's unit (thereby requiring an example to be made). If found guilty, the man's sentence would have to be approved by the chain of command with final authorization coming from the Commander-in-Chief.

The procedures for the execution were well laid out. The soldier's unit was responsible for carrying out the sentence and the convicted man could be attended by a chaplain, if desired. The soldier would be identified by a Non-Commissioned Officer of his unit before proceeding to the execution site. A stretcher would be provided if the convicted man could not walk.

A Firing Party of one officer, one sergeant and 10 soldiers would wait with their backs turned to the execution post. The prisoner would be brought to the place of execution, blindfolded and tied to the post or tree. The Medical Officer would fix a small paper disc over his heart.

The Firing Party would turn with five men standing and five men kneeling. One of the Firing Party's rifle (unknown) contained a blank. With the command, "Fire," the deed was done. The Medical Officer would inspect the man and pronounce him dead or, if still alive (which did occur), the officer in charge of the Firing Party would complete the sentence. The body would be removed for burial and the correct paperwork completed. A volunteer had died for his country.

For official purposes, the man would appear on the casualty lists as "died." If his next-of-kin asked for the particulars of the death, the officials would contact the clergy in the man's hometown. If the clergy believed the family, due to age or state of health, could not cope with the news, they would not be informed. Secrecy also helped the next-of-kin keep their social standing in the community. It is unknown how many families of the 25 Canadians executed were not informed of their son's or husband's execution.

Of the 25 Canadian soldiers executed, nine were from Arthur Currie's 1st Division, eight from the 2nd Division, two from Louis Lipsett's 3rd Division and three from David Watson's 4th Division. Statistics apparently suggest more compassion for their men from the Commanders of the 3rd and 4th Divisions. The other three soldiers belonged to Artillery, Cavalry and Army Service Corps. Four of the 25 men were not tried by the Canadians but by the British. In these cases, the Canadian Expeditionary Force was notified after the sentence was passed.

By battalion, five men of the 22nd Battalion (Canadien-français) and two men of the 3rd Battalion (Toronto Regiment) were executed. No other units had more than one executed.

This statistic seems to illustrate a bias against the French Canadians for, in addition, two French Canadians serving with other units were executed. The exaggerated disproportion possibly represents more than poor discipline in a fighting unit.

Political motivations may have played an important role in the death sentence given and duly carried out on Private Demetro Sinicky of the 52nd Battalion (Northern Ontario).

Sinicky was tried and convicted of cowardice in the face of the enemy. He had no previous convictions. His commanding officer presented no report and no record of recommendations regarding the carrying out of the death penalty.

Sinicky was Russian-born. After the Russian Revolution of 1917, paranoic fear spread through the Allied army concerning the rise of Bolshevism. A mutiny of Russian troops occurred in France. The Canadian Corps reacted by transferring many Russian-born soldiers from front-line units to the Railway Troops. Considering Sinicky's record, something else must have determined the death penalty.

Three Canadians were executed for desertion during the Battle of the Somme. Their trials are summarized below. Judge for yourself.

Private Henry Kerr, 7th Canadian Battalion

Tried November 7, 1916 for deserting His Majesty's Service

"The accused absented himself from the support trenches, after having been warned for the front line, and remained absent till found in billets, some miles in rear, twenty-four hours later, thereby avoiding a dangerous duty.

"The reports rendered by his platoon commander, his company commander and his commanding officer on this man's conduct were extremely bad. One one occasion in the trenches only on threat of being immediately shot would he leave his dugout to carry out his duties. So bad, indeed, was his example under shell fire that his comrades on the last occasion in the trenches at which the accused was present had asked that he might be left behind in future. It was also stated that he continually threatened to shoot officers and NCOs.

"All authorities concurred in recommending the carrying out of the death penalty."

Shot November 11, 1916.

Private Elsworth Young, 25th Canadian Battalion

Tried October 19, 1916 for deserting His Majesty's Service

"Accused was an officer's servant. On 16th September 1916 he was ordered to report to his Company Sergeant Major, who was then at Sausage Valley on way up to the line. (Heavy fighting was then in progress on the Somme). He did not do so. on 29th September he was arrested by the Military Police at Abbeville, a good many miles to the rear, disguised as a corporal of the Artillery and after having given false details about himself.

"Conduct sheet contained five entries, all relating to minor offences. There is no recommendation and report which is made by the Commanding Officer in all death penalty cases but in his evidence before the Court his CO said the accused had been with the battalion since 1914 and though he had been thoughtless and careless and was undependable nothing had previously been brought against him regarding his conduct in the line. Brigade Commander's recommendation in this case is also missing. Divisional Commander recommended commutation of sentence. Corps and Army Commanders disagreed on ground that offence was deliberate, in order to evade fighting and C-In-C confirmed."

Shot October 29, 1916. Aged 19.

Private John Higgins, 1st Canadian Battalion

Tried November 26, 1916 for deserting His Majesty's Service

"The accused left his platoon without orders when it was proceeding to the trenches during the fighting on the Somme and remained absent till apprehended by the French police behind the fighting area sixteen days later. After his arrest he escaped and remained absent till again apprehended five days later.

"Accused only had one trivial entry in his conduct sheet. His conduct up to the commission of the offence, both from a fighting point of view and from a point of behaviour, was reported by his commanding officer to have been satisfactory. Nevertheless, as the offence was deliberately committed to evade duty in the trenches his commanding officer and all higher authorities considered the sentence should stand."

Shot December 7, 1916. Aged 24.

FOR FURTHER REFERENCE

No battle of the First World War has been written about as much as the Battle of the Somme. Since the 1920s, books have been published about this campaign. It has a certain place in the ethos of the British mind-set and continues to captivate. Perhaps because of the catastrophic failure of the first day when 20,000 were killed, or perhaps it marks the end of an era in British history — it is still the centre of the First World War.

The same cannot be said of the Canadian participation. Books containing much more than a passing reference to the Canadians' involvement in the Battle of the Somme are rare.

Listed below are battlefields and books on the Somme that will be of interest. There is much to see on the Somme.

Do not miss:

The Thiepval Memorial to the Missing (lists 72,000 British soldiers with no known grave in the Somme area).

The South African National Memorial and Museum, Delville Wood.

Beaumont-Hamel Newfoundland Memorial Park is the best pre-served battlefield on the Western front. As Newfoundland did not join Canada until 1949, the Royal Newfoundland Regiment fought with British units during the war, suffering terrible casualties (one out of every four who enlisted died).

The Ulster Tower, Thiepval.

Lochnager Crater, La Boiselle.

The Tank Memorial, Pozières.

GUIDE BOOKS

Before Endeavours Fade by R. E. Coombs, Battle of Britain Prints International, 1976.

The Somme, Then and Now by J. Giles. Battle of Britain Prints International, 1986.

The Somme Battlefields by M. and M. Middlebrook. Viking, 1991.

ON THE BATTLE

The Somme by A. H. Farrar-Hockley. B. T. Batsford Ltd., 1966.

The Hell They Call High Wood by T. Norman. William Kimber & Co., 1984.

The First Day on the Somme by M. Middlebrook. Allen Lane, 1971.

Canada in Flanders Vol. III by Major C. G. D. Roberts. Hodder & Stoughton, 1918.

Delville Wood by I. Uys. Uys Publishers, 1983.

Somme by Lyn Macdonald. Michael Joseph Ltd., 1983.

The Grave of Pioneer E. C. Innes "For King and Country"

(PHOTO N. CHRISTIE)

Tour Map

The Canadians on the Somme
(September – November 1916)

(Simplified Trench Systems)

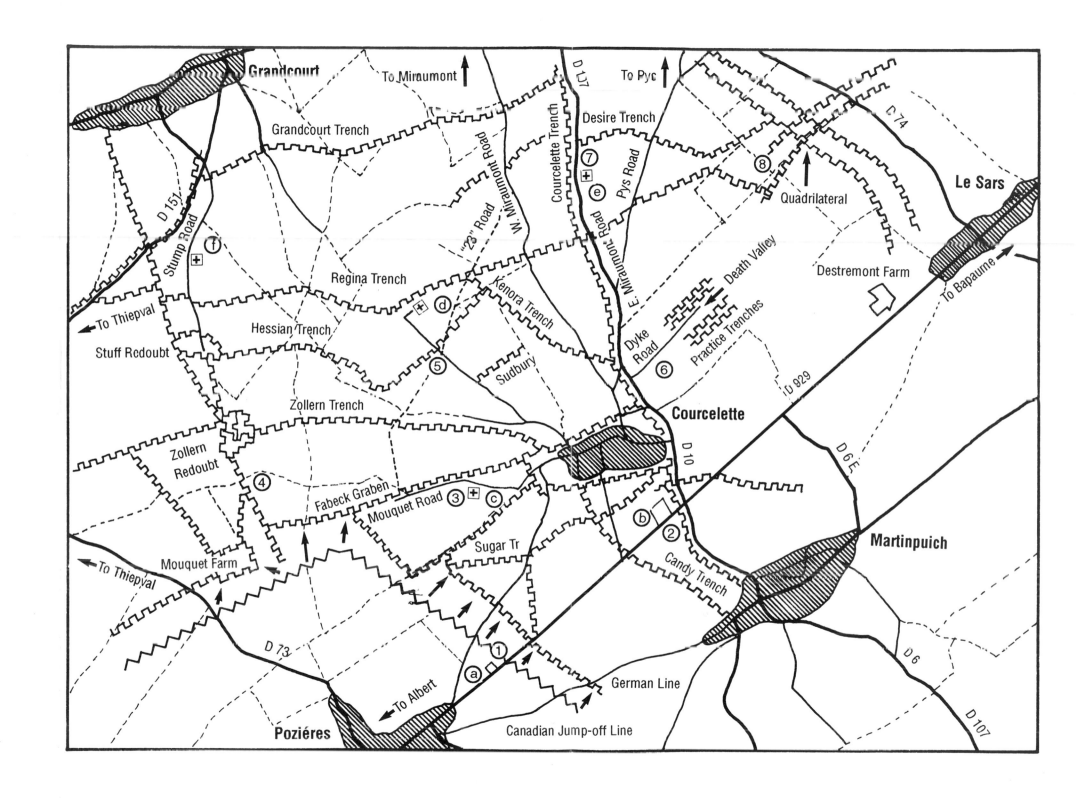

ⓐ	Australian Windmill Memorial
ⓑ	Canadian Memorial
ⓒ	Courcelette British Cemetery
ⓓ	Regina Trench Cemetery
ⓔ	Adanac Cemetery
ⓕ	Stump Road Cemetery
①	Tour Points

Scale 1km = 4cm

Grandcourt
To Miraumont
D 107
To Pys
Desire Trench
Le Sars
Grandcourt Trench
Courcelette Trench
D 74
⑦
⑧
Pys Road
ⓔ
Quadrilateral
D 151
"23" Road
W. Miraumont Road
Destremont Farm
Stump Road
Regina Trench
ⓕ
Kenora Trench
E. Miraumont Road
Death Valley
To Bapaume
ⓓ
To Thiepval
Hessian Trench
Practice Trenches
Stuff Redoubt
⑤
Sudbury
Dyke Road
⑥
D 929
Zollern Trench
Courcelette
Zollern Redoubt
④
Fabeck Graben
③ ⓒ
D 10
ⓑ
②
Mouquet Road
Martinpuich
Mouquet Farm
To Thiepval
Sugar Tr
D 6E
Candy Trench
D 6
D 73
①
To Albert
ⓐ
German Line
D 107
Poziéres
Canadian Jump-off Line